Born in 1959 in Hemel Hempstead, Dougie Brimson went directly into the RAF from school where he trained as a mechanical engineer. After serving for over eighteen years and attaining the rank of sergeant, he left the forces in 1994 to pursue a career as a writer. He is married to Tina (a lapsed Hammer) and has three children.

Eddy Brimson was also born in Hemel Hempstead, in 1964, and after leaving school, he trained as a graphic designer. He is married to Harriet, a Gooner!

The Brimsons are the authors of two previous books, *Everywhere We Go* and *England, My England* – both of which were published by Headline in 1996.

Dedication

This book could only have been written with the help and support of Tina, Harriet and the family.

With special thanks to all at Headline and all those who helped us out and supported us in any way.

It is written for all those supporters who lived and loved the great game in the days before it became fashionable and who will still be with it when the bubble bursts.

Keep the faith, lads, and *Up the 'Ornets!*

And for Felix.

Capital Punishment

London's Violent Football Following

Dougie and Eddy Brimson

HEADLINE

First published in 1997
by HEADLINE BOOK PUBLISHING

10 9 8 7 6 5 4 3

ISBN 0 7472 5713 2

Typeset by Avon Dataset Ltd, Bidford-on-Avon, Warks

Printed and bound in Great Britain by
Mackays of Chatham PLC, Chatham, Kent

HEADLINE BOOK PUBLISHING
A division of Hodder Headline PLC
338 Euston Road
London NW1 3BH

Contents

Introduction
London Calling

There is absolutely no doubt whatsoever that London is *the* centre of football in England. The residents of Liverpool, Newcastle or Manchester may well get the hump with that statement but tough shit, look at the facts. Using the M25 as a guide, there are within its confines fourteen league clubs, a figure that cannot be matched by any other region. Add to that the fact that the national stadium and the FA headquarters at Lancaster Gate are also within the same boundary and the case is as clear as L*t*n are shit. There is of course an argument that 90 per cent of the really successful teams are up north, but we southerners choose to ignore that.

Having so many teams within an hour's drive is, not to put too fine a point on it, 'Lovely Jubbly'. For those who live inside the M25, it means that not only do they have any number of local derby games, less travelling and more drinking, but if their own teams are not playing, they will not have that far to travel to find another game. Furthermore, if England are playing then Wembley is just up the road and you can get back home again in time to watch the highlights on telly. London, as far as football is concerned, is the only place to live.

For those in charge of football, the downside of this is that for those supporters who enjoy a bit of a ruck – and yes, there are still the odd thousand around – the number of local derbies provides ample opportunity to play up. What is more, the fact that any number of clubs' supporters will be coming into, or just passing through London on matchdays means that the chance to settle the odd score, or merely cause a bit of mayhem, will come around fairly quickly. Similarly, any of the more active groups involved in an ongoing feud with another London side may not even bother to wait until the fixture comes around before escalating things, something which has been seen on countless occasions and which the Metropolitan Police are quick to acknowledge. London on a Saturday afternoon, or a Tuesday night, can be a rough place to be if you're a footie fan.

It is our intention within these pages to look at the background of hooliganism in the capital. We will be looking at all of the London clubs, even Wimbledon, but everyone must acknowledge that there are three which stand out: Chelsea, West Ham and Millwall. Inevitably, these clubs are covered in more detail than the rest as we look back at the history of the 'firms' associated with them, groups such as the ICF, the Headhunters and the F-Troop, as well as some of the more infamous incidents they are known to have been actively involved in. We will also examine the way that these groups use London and its travel network in order to ambush their opponents and fool the police.

As in our previous books, an integral part of *Capital Punishment* will be first-hand accounts of such incidents. Some of them come from those we either know or have met, others from those who have chosen to write to us, but they are all, as usual, reproduced verbatim. We have done this because we believe that the impact and consequences of this violence come across far stronger this way than if we were to dress them up in the Queen's English.

What this book is not, however, is a glowing endorsement of either hooliganism or London as a hot-bed of football violence. While we have focused on the London clubs individually, not all the accounts included are about them 'getting a result'. There are plenty of clubs in other parts of the country for whom a visit to London is as good an excuse as any to indulge in mayhem. Those groups relish the thought of possible confrontation with any bunch of 'Cockney Wankers' and have on many occasions come to the capital and run the London firms on their own patch. Reputation is everything to the hooligan groups, whether they are well-organised or not, and 'doing London' is one way of putting yourself on the map. That is why, for the hooligan, London is so fascinating.

It is not our intention within *Capital Punishment* to examine in detail those issues, like the role of the police, the FA, media; etc, in football, that we covered in our previous books.

However, the truth, as far as we are concerned, is that going to football these days is far less enjoyable than it was when we were 'at it' in the seventies and eighties. It is nothing to do with the fact that we no longer indulge in hooliganism, nor anything to do with the fact that Watford are viewed as a sleeping midget, playing crap football. It is to do with the fact that the atmosphere at games has changed, and football at far too many grounds has lost that unique mixture of passion and hostility which made the English game so special.

If you are lucky enough to visit Stamford Bridge, you will notice that that passion remains and makes the place almost unique in the Premier League. Yet Old Trafford, Highbury, White Hart Lane, and even to a lesser extent Anfield, have lost it and the atmosphere on most match days is almost bland by comparison. This is almost entirely due to the fact that the FA and the clubs themselves, in a misguided quest to change the game's fan-base, has sought to dilute the traditional vocal-male element with an influx of new-wave, trendy fans who simply do not know how to create a half-decent atmosphere. It may have removed much of the violence from the stadia, but with it went the atmosphere; and in any case, the violence may have left the grounds for now but it certainly hasn't disappeared.

Condemn the hooligans as much as you like, but not every group of lads was out to cause a row; yet the football authorities tarred all vocal, passionate males with the same brush. They started to pander to every group bar the main bulk of their support, the blokes. Geezers create an atmosphere that the suits, women and children will never be able to generate.

To say that the explosion of hooliganism in the seventies and eighties was killing football is only half the story, an easy cop-out for those that mismanaged the game. Crowds were falling because with a few exceptions such as Liverpool, Arsenal and Forest, the standard of football was crap. For every so-called classic game you see on the nostalgic football programmes, how many awful ones did we have to endure? Furthermore, the stadia and facilities were terrible and people began to wake up to alternative entertainment industries that were falling over themselves to treat the customer with something football never did, respect.

It is clear to us that football at the top level is storing up huge problems for itself and seems to be ignorant of the likely consequences. As the top clubs continue to chase the consumers with the fattest wallets, they seem totally unconcerned that the smaller clubs are starting to go under. Where is the new talent going to come from? Continue to purchase cheap European players, by all means; but don't then turn around and tell us that the national side are shit and that the game in this country is being left behind.

Leaving aside the continuing obsession with foreign players taking money out of the domestic game, look at the stranglehold on football being exerted by television, which is the real threat to our game. The Premier League seems hell-bent on bringing in pay-per-view, and the repercussions of that for lesser clubs will be considerable. For example, we know that many Chelsea, Tottenham and Arsenal fans have allegiances to, and from time to time go to watch, some of the smaller clubs within the capital (something not unique to London fans, as many supporters throughout the country have a 'second team'). With pay-per-view and the opportunity to buy a season ticket for their own front-room, those floating fans may just decide to stay at home instead, taking much-needed revenue from the Leyton Orient or Barnet bank accounts. Already while overall attendances have generally risen in recent years, crowds in the bottom two divisions have tended to be lower since the existence of the Premier League.

Those who travelled will now be able to stay at home, and for those on a budget, sitting at home watching Coventry play Southampton at The Dell is infinitely preferable to, and cheaper than, travelling to watch it live. It means that fewer people will be going to watch football in the flesh, and that means even less revenue at the gate. Some may argue that as you have to buy your decoder to access the TV, football will benefit, but as you can get ten people in my front-room to watch a game, simple mathematics tells me that the clubs will be losing out.

The other danger with pay-per-view is that we will see a massive growth in the 'pub football' culture that satellite TV has started to produce. As was seen when England were knocked out of Euro 96, the possibility for violence here is immense. Football, alcohol and men have never mixed that well, and we have already heard of mobs attacking pubs containing rival fans that are many miles away from the actual fixture. Within the capital, there are exiled supporters' clubs for almost every side in the country. Once clubs such as Burnley start to find their 'home' pub, the historical 'taking of the end' will be replaced by the 'taking of the pub', and as any active hooligan already knows, it's at the pubs and clubs that most of the battles increasingly occur.

It's a very real threat and one which the football authorities won't address, because they can distance themselves from this kind of violence – any trouble in pubs showing games live can be put down to 'our violent society' rather than football, with the cost picked up by the taxpayer, not the game. But by watching the game on television, people get out of the habit of going to matches and once you lose that habit it is difficult to go back. Ask the Exeters and the Hull Citys how they will feel when their gates are down because the Merseyside derby is available live in people's front-rooms or showing down the local pub.

The continuing alienation of supporters from their clubs, and the refusal to listen to their views and/or genuine complaints, is another cause for concern. One only has to look at Brighton to see how wrong things can go once matters get out of hand, and how it is the supporters who suffer the real consequences. The authorities have refused to accept that supporters who turn up to matches are an essential part of the game and see most of us as nothing more than a milk cow. Many clubs now make great play of the fact that people walking through the turnstiles actually generate less than half of their income, yet they talk about that as if 'half' is an insignificant amount. This assumption is total bollocks anyway; add the money spent on food, drink, club lotteries and in the club shop on match days and all of a sudden, that 'half' is growing. It would appear that football has the same people juggling the figures as the government have when talking about unemployment or the NHS!

Clubs also have to accept that they have a responsibility too, for the well-being and behaviour of their supporters both at home and away. Their continuing refusal to accept this responsibility is itself causing anger among supporters who, in many instances, suffer at the hands of the police or the opposing fans. The Millwall directors were screaming blue murder about the behaviour of Birmingham City fans when they visited St Andrews, holding them totally responsible for the events that took place. Yet when Millwall fans go for it at the New Den, the club has much less to say for itself. You can't have it both ways, can you?

The truth of the matter is that as far as the BBC, the Premier League and the FA are concerned, there is no life outside the Premiership and it is being marketed as such to a different breed of football fan, the ones who watch the game at home. Those who sit in the rain and cold or spend their hard-earned money travelling around the country are simply ignored. Yet every supporter who was watching football before Sky, and those of us who watch the game at the lower levels, know that nothing has changed. The threat of violence persists. The concerted effort by the media moguls to keep the darker side of football off our screens and out of the newspapers doesn't mean that Chelsea, Tottenham, Man United, Liverpool and every other Premier League club has not experienced violence within their stadium confines this season; they all have, prove us wrong if you dare. It hasn't gone away, and what happens when the new family-unit commodity finally comes across this dinosaur from the past?

As for the two of us, we remain committed to doing anything we can to help solve the continuing problem of hooliganism at football in this country. We do this because as former hooligans, we feel compelled to put something back into the game which we, in the past, damaged by our actions. As long as football continues to turn its back on the fans, deny the problem still exists and bleed us, the fans, dry, we will continue to write books such as this to highlight their ignorance. The sanitised version of football that we see on *Match of the Day* and *Super Sunday* seems very different when you're faced with a mob of opposing fans intent on kicking the shit out of you and the very real threat of hooliganism is suddenly there in your face. When the game finally wakes up to that, then we may actually see some real headway made in this ongoing battle.

PART ONE
Capital Punishment

Chapter 1 *Why?*

Chapter 1
Why?

Whenever I, Eddy, speak to people about football violence, I get the same old question and comments. 'What was it all about?' . . . 'You strike me as being quite an intelligent bloke!' . . . 'WHY?' Usually those question are asked by people who don't really want to hear the answers. DJs wanting to be controversial, 'Not 'arf, listeners.' Newspaper reporters responding to the latest outbreak and looking for someone to point the finger at, or people who have never been to a game in their lives but know all the answers. Well, let's try to clear it up once and for all and explain just what being a football hooligan meant to me.

We have said over and over again that if people didn't like fighting they wouldn't do it, but being a football hooligan involved much more than just the violence. When I first became involved it was all very sporadic, happening just now and then, but by the time I had finished it had changed dramatically and become a whole movement. I became a football hooligan in the same way that other people become punks, skins, mods or bikers, and I did my growing up on the terraces of England and Europe.

No one ever forced me into going to football and getting involved in its darker side. As a young kid, I found it unbelievably exciting to see my best friend's brother and his mates go steaming across a terrace, flares and fists flying as 50-odd away fans ran and huddled down in the corner by the tea hut. Every now and then the away fans would stand their ground and fight back, and the police would charge in and take people away to God knows where. The troops would then return bloodied and bruised but with heads held high. I used to stand and stare with an 'I know him, that's my mate's brother, that is' look upon my face as those standing beside me cheered the lads on. I wanted to be part of that and I knew that one day I would experience the battle for myself. When that day finally arrived, I felt like I could have taken on the world and that was a feeling I relived again and again.

Don't patronise me by saying that I wasn't a true supporter or follower of the game. I could tell you the score, the goalscorer and how he scored it from every game I ever attended. I was, and still am, football-mad. I could probably even give you the attendance figures at those games, but I could also supply a list of the pitches I ran onto. I don't say that with any great pride, but it's not meant as an apology either and I certainly don't regret any of it.

Following as I did a club like Watford, most of the memories linked to the violence seem to involve getting away without getting battered! But taking liberties on other people's turf, running Brentford down at the Junction, getting bitten by a police dog at Everton, being well turned-over at Oxford and coming home from Arsenal with a fat lip and a black eye are all memories that bring a smile to my face and make me think back to the good old days – because to me that is exactly what they were, all of them, even the hidings; fucking marvellous. I know that there will be plenty of people disgusted at what I've just written. Reporters, DJs and researchers will be reaching for their high-lighter pens; maybe Kilroy might even give us a call, who knows? But to me it was just part of growing up, real life and amazingly exciting. I belonged to something which took me away from the average person's day-to-day life and put me in the firing line. It could be dangerous and it was in-your-face. Just as some people try Bungee-jumping or parachuting once or twice in their life in order to get the adrenaline buzz that danger brings, so I went to The Den, Anfield or St James' Park (in both Newcastle and

Exeter). Every Saturday was different and you never knew what was waiting for you around the next corner.

I have spent many hours listening to older men and women talk about the Bank Holiday riots between the police, the mods and the rockers at Southend or Brighton. Those days are recalled as great memories from their past, as they chased and got chased by each other while sending startled nans and grandads running for cover. They would look forward to the Bank Holidays for weeks on end and, in their local pub or club, the group would plan their annual away days. These pubs and clubs were seen as home territory. If any group turned up and started taking liberties, things would often turn nasty as defence of that territory became all-important. All these movements were linked to a certain kind of music, and for them the gigs were just another outlet for possible violence. At almost every punk gig you expected skin-heads to turn up and kick things off. At the mod gigs around the home counties in the early eighties, fighting would always break out between rival gangs of scooter boys out to prove themselves and get the best birds.

All this starts to sound very familiar. The concerts/match days, the clubs/home ends, and the Bank Holiday trips/away games. Identifying the bikers and the punks was easy, as they all had their uniform. Unfortunately, for the football hooligan it was the silk scarf, pie-crust shoes or steel-toe-capped Doc Martens and flares (it's painful to look back on, I know). Then like a bolt from above came the casual look, clean-cut and expensive, releasing us all from high-waisters trousers with side-pockets forever, and giving us an identity we had never previously enjoyed. Long live the casual!

Up until the birth of the casual movement, which was so strong in London, most football mobs would have people of all descriptions running with them. It didn't matter what you looked like as long as you were prepared to stand your ground and fight it out. Once the casuals came into being, all that changed. There was no way that you could tolerate a long-haired, pizza-faced bloke wearing an Iron Maiden T-shirt and baseball boots any longer, it was take-a-shower-or-sod-off time. Either you were in or you were out, and in those days being in meant being smart, being clean, wearing top gear and being up for it.

What the casual movement also did was take the violence to a different level. There had always been firms with their leaders and top boys, but now that the football hooligan had a clear identity, mobs were turning up everywhere. As they became more and more organised, firms were adopting names for themselves, giving an even greater sense of identity. You had to let people know who you were if you wanted to build a reputation, and building a reputation for the firm was what it was all about. There was only one way you could do that. It didn't matter what anyone else thought or said, we knew the rules. I belonged to something, as did thousands of other blokes throughout the country, and to me this was fantastic.

Arriving for the match on a Saturday in the wrong gear made you a laughing stock for the whole day. You *had* to be seen wearing the right label. The feeling of walking down the road, dressed-up and looking the dog's bollocks, was fucking fantastic. The casuals did away with wearing the club colours, a move that many didn't like. They saw it as a cop-out that made it easy to hide away when the going got tough, but we saw it as an ideal way of being able to infiltrate police escorts, away ends and other firms. Actually, the only people we were fooling were the police, because any football hooligan can spot the opposition a mile off and in those days the clothes were a dead giveaway as to who and what you were about.

Yes, we were angry, aggressive and violent; but unlike the punks, skins or bikers, we weren't rebelling against anything. We had no statement to make against society, we just loved to put ourselves over as flash bastards that didn't give a toss. We didn't care about anything other than finding another group of blokes exactly the same as ourselves and beating the shit out of each other, and we were only interested in other casuals. We had money in our pockets and were doing very nicely, thank you; yet there we were, wanting to smash the fuck out of the opposition while wearing more money on our backs than most of the people around us earned in a month.

Why?

Pringle, Fila, Diadora, Tacchini, Lacoste, etc – what a uniform it was, good expensive clothing. If it got ruined, then it would be back down the West End or maybe even a late-night visit to the local golf-course shop. To say that a lot of us had long pockets in those days would be a major understatement. Being a casual could prove to be an expensive hobby, and many of our lads would catch a midweek train to Euston with a shopping list as long as your arm and no money. Early evening, you would make the call to see if your request had been successful; if not, then you would find out what else was on offer and how much it would set you back, but with Saturday just around the corner you had to be wearing something new.

I remember once following some Birmingham City fans being escorted back to Watford Junction after an evening home game and the opposing casuals soon sussing us out. There was no chance of it going off because the police at Watford were right on top of it, but contact had been made. As we gave each other the usual verbal, the Brummies were showing great interest in some of the clothes we were wearing, particularly one of our lads' jackets which they told us they wanted to relieve him of. Once up on the platform, it was clear that this little firm had come from Milton Keynes and were going back on the same slow train as us, not with the main bulk of the Brummie fans. They piled on at one end as we got on at the other. The train pulled into Hemel Hempstead and we got off as normal, then all of a sudden the City fans jumped off and came steaming at us, running across the track and over the fence out of the station. All the City fans were shouting, 'Get the bloke in the jacket!' That's the way it was then; not only did they want to batter us, they wanted to nick all our gear as well.

We all got away unscathed, but as the Brummies had to wait for the next train, this gave us enough time to get tooled-up and pay a return visit. We got well run that night, but at least one of them went home with a little reminder after being floored following a shower of bottles and bricks as we forced them back into the station and up onto the platform.

By the mid-eighties, our firm had really fallen apart. The likes of West Ham and Chelsea had visited once too often, and I could no longer stand the taunting that the children's TV programme *Murphy's Mob* brought to what was left of our reputation. But the football hooligan fan-culture still fascinated me and has done to this day. Football hooligans have an amazing attitude towards each other that many can't figure out. I remember travelling to Newcastle and coming across a firm of Sunderland at a service station. Again, I thought we were in for a right hiding, but once they sussed out that we were on our way to play their main rivals, they gave us all the information they could about the way the United firm worked. This saved us from turning up the wrong road and helped us to have a little bit of a result of our own, well away from their main lads. You see, we all belonged to the same movement. You could usually get on with anyone unless you were actually playing them.

Another aspect of the hooligan movement is that, unlike almost any other scene, it is totally male. We all know that groups consisting entirely of only males (or females) act differently when the opposite sex are out of sight. I would never have got involved in a fight away from football, but being part of a mob gave me the chance to prove myself against other men and I loved that. I love being a bloke and I like to be with other blokes, talking bollocks, cracking jokes and putting the world to rights. Football gave me the chance to do all those things. It also provided an outlet for me to do all the ugly things that some men get up to like swearing, fighting and being a complete pain in the arse just for the sake of it, and all out of view of the girlfriend. I am convinced that is why so many people continue to be involved in the violence even when they get much older. It's a male thing, a way in which to express your manhood.

I am not in any way trying to defend or excuse myself as a 'poor old misunderstood ex-football hooligan'. Make no mistake, I loved it. I feel no need to justify what I did, because I am not ashamed of it. The truth is that we come from a sound upbringing, enjoyed school and college, and do not fit the image of the football hooligan that the media quite wrongly portray but quite rightly love to hate. Being part of any such movement means that you don't give a fuck what anyone on the outside thinks of you; my only concern at that time was what those I ran with thought. When the use of weapons started to come into it, though, I thought it was time to jump ship. I didn't mind the odd fat lip, but I really didn't fancy looking in the mirror every day at a false smile I never even wanted. I saw some terrible incidents in my time, and believe me I ran with a firm that didn't come anywhere near the big boys.

Indeed, by the time the all-seater stadium came around I had turned my back on football. Both the game and the way in which the supporter was able to watch it were starting to change dramatically. As a supporter, I had no say in the way they ran the game and that made me angry – just because I liked the odd row didn't mean I knew nothing about football. Ultimately I turned my back on the game for three or four seasons, attending only a handful of home matches. Looking at football and the way it is today, I feel exactly the same: I am being screwed. But you can't stay away forever and now you will find me at every home game as well as a few away fixtures.

That break enabled me to cut myself off from the hooligan element and finally throw my Ellesse trainers in the bin. There are very few people involved in the mob at the club today that I could even name. Many of the old faces from the other little mobs around during my time are still going, but like me they keep their distance, most of the time. The casual movement is on its way back, though a few of the labels have changed. Now it's Ralph Lauren, Stone Island, Henri Lloyd and Armani, but the feeling I am sure is the same for these lads as it was for me, and I can't help watching and thinking of the old days.

I am sure that many men find much better ways in which to express themselves, but football and football violence did it for me and I know it continues to do the same for many others. If you were ever one of those mods or rockers at Brighton, a punk, a skin or whatever, you may just understand a bit of what being a football casual meant to me. If you have tried Bungee-jumping and felt that buzz, you will also understand the thrill that comes through danger.

Chapter 2
The North–South Divide

Before we become entrenched in the football side of things, it is important that we have a quick look at the different areas of London. To the average southerner, this may seem a strange thing to do but remember, those from outside the M25 call all Londoners Cockneys because as far as they are concerned, we are. We even get the old Cockney tag at Watford – are we bollocks! Mind you, that's no different from us calling everyone else northerners, sheep-shaggers, carrot-crunchers, Geordies, etc.

As two blokes of North London extraction (Tottenham actually) we should have a spiritual bond with that area, but we must stress that we have no loyalty to the clubs who play there. This is almost entirely due to the influence of our old man, who spent our formative years boring us rigid with tales of how brilliant Spurs were in the fifties and how great they are today. Now the nearest he comes to watching them is when *we* tell him how they got on, and he wouldn't know Darren Anderton (who actually lives only round the corner from him) if he ran him over. This almost certainly drove us to rebel against him and suffer many seasons supporting the Hornets. But then again, they are our local club.

London can be split into five geographical areas: North, South, East, West and the City itself. Which parts of London fall into which region is often a matter of fierce debate among its population, but as far as we are concerned, North London is from the

19

River Lea round to Mill Hill; West London from Mill Hill over the Thames and down to Kingston; South London from Wimbledon and Morden round to the A2, taking in all that is south of the river; and East London consists of everything north of the river east of Stepney, Leyton and Chingford. The City, or Square Mile, is the relatively small area in the middle around Bank tube, and in footballing terms is only relevant because it's where the directors will go when they put your club on the Stock Exchange (the final nail in the coffin). The fact that the Millwall area is north of the river and the New Den lies to the south in New Cross causes some confusion, but the 'Lions' are as much a part of the East End as Grant Mitchell and will always be regarded as such. Similarly, as most people know, true Cockneys were born within the sound of Bow Bells and there are actually very few real Cockneys left.

The different areas of London have always had specific accents and characteristics and, like the different regions of most cities, a pretty healthy distrust of everywhere else. The East End, spiritual home of the Cockney, has always had, along with the traditional East End wit, a violent and aggressive undercurrent. This was something that originated from the docks and from the fact that many of the poorest areas of the city could be found in the region. As a result, the East End population and its football clubs have been saddled with this 'rough' image, and to a certain extent it is a pretty fair reflection. While the Kray twins were hardly the typical East End family of the fifties and sixties, you got the general idea. Similarly, West London was always regarded as the flash part of the city and has invariably been home to the trendy set and most of London's entertainment. Again, this is reflected in the clubs, especially Chelsea and QPR who have always had the same sort of flash and brash image, as have their supporters. South of the river has always been a bit dodgy to those who don't live there, and even now, the two of us feel a bit wary when we cross a bridge over the Thames. We have absolutely no doubt that most people who live across the water are shifty and untrustworthy; whenever you saw one of the old 'spivs' so prevalent in old Ealing comedies, he almost certainly came from Lambeth,

Bermondsey or somewhere like that. Never, ever buy a car or household appliance from someone willing to admit to coming from this area. One only has to look at Crystal Palace to prove the point; no class and a bit shady.

As lads from North London stock, we have to say that this is the area of London where you will find the most friendly and hospitable members of its population. They may appear cocky and arrogant to some, but we have to say this otherwise we will be eaten alive the next time we visit our relatives. The fact that Spurs and Arsenal, like them or loathe them, have been the most successful London clubs over the years must also be pointed out.

Following the Second World War, London, and especially the East End, required massive rebuilding. This eventually led to a large portion of the population leaving the city and moving out into the suburbs, where housing and employment were more readily available. However, those who moved retained a fierce loyalty to their city roots and to their respective football clubs, and this has been passed down through the generations. Certainly, if you walk around Romford or Grays – both areas east of London – the wearing of anything other than claret-and-blue would be ill-advised. Indeed, for many in those towns, West Ham shirts are obligatory dress in the summer months and this pattern is repeated west of London – where Greenford, Staines, etc, are full of Chelsea and QPR – and north of the city in the New Towns such as Stevenage and our own home, Hemel Hempstead, which was once full of Spurs and Arsenal fans. Now, due to TV, it could be Man United or Liverpool. In addition to these traditional links, the growth of television and the widespread availability of replica kits has seen support for all of London's major clubs, as well as those from much further afield, spread throughout the region.

As the 'old' population left London, the void was filled by a huge influx of immigrants who sadly, and for numerous reasons, have often tended to stay away from football. The clubs themselves are well aware of this and many are actively involved in their communities in a bid to attract new local support and spread the word. We applaud that work and wish it every success, but in this book our interest lies with those supporters who already go to football and, more specifically, those who go and sometimes become involved in trouble. The fact that they all support London clubs is their only common link because other than that, little love is lost between any of them.

If the fans of most London clubs have problems with each other, it is fair to say that Londoners in general are hardly the most popular group of people in Britain. Those who live anywhere north of Northampton tend to regard Londoners as cocky, flash and arrogant – which is pretty fair, really. After all, many southerners in turn tend to regard most northerners as thick, most Geordies as mad and most Scousers as thieves; stereotyping at its worst. Our own experiences have taught us that while northerners who come to London tend to play down their accents and mannerisms – something almost entirely due to the fact that they usually go to the West End, which is full of tourists anyway – when southerners, and in particular Londoners, are up north, then they tend to play up to their stereotype with great pride. Certainly back in the seventies and eighties, a trip up north was a great excuse to get all cocky as most Londoners suddenly turned into Del Boy.

'There is no way that I am going to let some northern ponce come down to my manor and take liberties.'

What a great quote that is. Maybe a bit offensive, maybe a bit arrogant, maybe total bollocks, it all depends on where you come from – but there can be no doubt that it echoes the feelings of many of the capital's football hooligans. As far as they are concerned, if you support a club that isn't on the tube map then you are nothing, two-bob.

Maybe the impression given below, describing anyone living outside the M25, sheds even more light on what those chirpy Cockneys think of the rest of the country.

MAYBE IT'S BECAUSE I'M A LONDONER

Now don't get me wrong, I know loads of northerners and admittedly the odd one is all right. But when it comes to having it off at football, they just don't cut it. Let's face it, northerners are wankers. They're clueless. I wouldn't trust one as far as I could throw him, but worst of all is that northerners, and everyone else for that matter, have got no bottle. Ask yourself, when was the last time any firm from outside the capital seriously came down mobbed-up and ready to take on any of the top London firms? See what I mean? Wankers.

They may come and give it the big 'un at Palace and Rangers but Mickey Mouse clubs don't count, it means nothing. Now that really pisses us off because we know they have the lads, of course they have. There are plenty of top firms around the country well able to hold their own and having it away every week. Well, what I say is, fucking bring it down here, we'd love to get it on. You see, that's the problem. They can do it on their own patch but will they ever come down here? Will they bollocks. We've taken it to them so many times it's got boring now.

Take Stoke, the Naughty Forty. Well up for it, a very tidy firm and well busy, but when it came to Millwall they fucked it. It's always the same. Everyone and his dog knew what was planned, even my nan asked if I was going down the New Den out of interest – she worries about me, you see. The Filth were all over them before they got past Coventry and that was that, end of story. Well, sorry lads, that's no way to do it, is it? You see, it's always easy to give it the large one when the Old Bill are there to keep the natives at bay; and as for the Zulu Army, well . . . 400 mums and dads is hardly a firm. Maybe next time, eh?

In my time I've had it away with firms from almost every club in the country you could mention, and I'll tell you, I've taken loads of hidings – but it won't stop me from going, because to be top dogs you have to be prepared to take the odd kicking. Londoners are prepared for that, and that is why the top firms in the country are all from the capital, Chelsea, West Ham and Millwall.

No one likes taking a hiding, and I don't leave my front door on a Saturday to go out and have the shit kicked out of me. But if something has been sorted, it's more than our reputation is worth to not turn up, and nine times out of ten that's enough. You don't get the excuses with the London firms. If someone is giving it the large one or on the way up, then we'll go there; from then on, it's up to them to take it to us. If they do, fair play, let's have it – but nine times out of ten it's all mouthy northern bollocks.

It's exactly the same if – and I mean if, because it doesn't happen very often – they come down here. Then we have to see they don't take liberties, that's the game. Unfortunately, it's all a bit one-sided at the moment.

You hear stories every week about what's happening around the country. Carlisle are doing this, Barnsley and West Brom did that. Well, yeah, right-oh, it all sounds good and I ain't saying it ain't true, but it's all a bit second-rate. Take Sheffield United, I had the shit kicked out of me up there a few years back, nasty bastards. So we gave them the chance to come down and see what they were made of away from their own patch and surprise, surprise, they never showed.

Personally, I think there are only two, maybe three firms outside of the capital that would have the bottle and the numbers for it, and that's Glasgow Rangers, Celtic and possibly Aberdeen. That would be something. Both Rangers and Celtic have well-tidy firms and that, added to the England–Scotland thing, would be sure to set it off. Even then, I don't know how long it would last. It's easy to take on the likes of Hibs and Dundee every now and then, but coming down here three, four times in a season would really let us know what they were made of. Aberdeen put up a good show during the European Championships, that could be a good one as well. We would love the chance to take it up there – new territory, lovely.

I've noticed that some of the larger northern firms haven't had the bottle for the Sweaties when they have met. Leeds kept themselves very quiet when they played Rangers a few years back. Sunderland, Villa, Burnley, they have all been turned over by Rangers, and Celtic gave the Zulu Army a fair run at Birmingham. I don't think they would get off so easily down here but, unlike everyone else, I am sure they would give it a good go. The Old Bill wouldn't know what to do, it would be mental. Maybe that's why we haven't got a British League yet, it could all go back to the good old days again.

You see, Cockneys are number one and to be number one you have to take on the best. I'm not just on about the football here, but it's only natural to want to better yourself in life. Everyone wants that, and that is why northerners, Sweaties, sheep-shaggers, carrot-crunchers, the lot, all really wish they were Cockneys as well. I mean, look at the facts. How many northerners, Paddys and Jocks do you know that came down to London for the weekend and ended up living here for the rest of their lives? Fucking loads! Then they have the nerve to go on about the shite beer, the birds, what it's like back home and house prices. Well, sorry we don't like shitting in the shed down here. We have a bit of class, and if it's really that good back home then why not take your tripe, haggis and spuds with you and sod off back to where you belong, simple. You don't get many Londoners going in the other direction, do you? Exactly.

Londoners may find it hard to believe but not every Englishman wants to be a Cockney. Some actually don't even like them. Terry from Rotherham explains:

SOFT SOUTHERN SHITE

Cockneys make me die. What the fuck do they think they are? Eh, really? All the London clubs think they're the bollocks; they're fuck all, mate.

All you need to be a Cockney is a leather jacket, a knife, a loud mouth and a good pair of running shoes. I've seen the backs of more Cockneys than a prozzie's seen ceilings.

Everyone goes on about Chelsea, West Ham and Millwall.

What about Man City, Forest, Middlesbrough, Stoke? There are more top firms in Yorkshire than in London. Leeds, Huddersfield, both the Sheffield firms, Bradford, even Barnsley are on the up now. London v Yorkshire, now that would be something. I tell you, they'd get their fucking arses kicked up here.

Another thing with Cockneys is that most of them ain't Cockneys at all, they come from middle-class, soft-as-shit suburbia. They don't know how to enjoy themselves 'cos they're too busy keeping up with the family next door.

When you follow England all you get is Chelsea this, Chelsea that. Where the fuck were they during Euro 96? I'll tell you: they were sitting in the corner of a pub giving it the big one when the rest of the country's lads were out giving it to the Jocks and the police. It wasn't the London lads doing all the work in Italy, Poland, Holland and Dublin, not by a long way, but all the press want is London. Well, fuck them, they can have it. The people that matter know what really goes on.

The London mobs have the tube in London; admittedly they know how to use it but they don't stand and fight, just hit and run. Any lads can do that, that's not hard. Standing and scrapping it out is hard. Cockney bollocks.

Most people in this country show some kind of pride in their place of birth, even Scousers. Being described as something they clearly are not can make some people a little upset, as was told to us by Dave B.

I AIN'T NO NORTHERNER, HONEST

I was born in North London in 1964 into a family that was West Ham mad, and my Dad started taking me when I was just five.

Unfortunately, when I was nine we had to move to the Midlands due to my Dad's work, but the Hammers had become a big part of my life and he was not going to let our

Cockney roots be forgotten – 'Remember son, you're London, always will be' – and whenever we made the trip down to see the relatives, it was always planned around a home game.

I enjoyed the fact that I was the only Hammers fan at my school, and the Cup final win over Fulham lifted me to celebrity status at the age of eleven.

When I got into my teens, Dad trusted me to make my own way back to my Nan's and would leave me after the game to go for a few jars with his old mates. At that time the violence was at its height and it was something that was part of the day-out at Upton Park. To kids of my age it often went unnoticed and Dad was never the type to get involved himself, but to me it was something that took away the boredom of the half-time break. Then one day, something happened that very nearly stopped me from ever going to a game again.

On my way home I would always stop at the chippy. I used to dream about those chips and looked forward to them as much as the match sometimes, they just ain't the same anywhere else. As usual, the place was packed and buzzing with the post-match talk. Finally it came to me to be served and I ordered the usual, large chips and a gherkin. I walked out the door, staring at the portion of lard that was warming my hands, when I suddenly felt a thump in my back. I turned around to see three kids about the same age as me who had also been in the chippy.

'You fucking northern bastard, you can't come in our chippy. We're going to kick your fucking head in for that.' At first it didn't register at all and I was looking around to see who they were talking to. 'You better start running, mate, 'cos we're going to kill you if you don't. Go on, fucking run.'

I remember replying and as I did so, the realisation hit me. 'I ain't a northerner, I was born in Ilford.' The words spurted out in a Brummie accent, I was doomed. I had never considered myself to be anything but a Londoner and still don't, but to these lads out to prove themselves I was northern through and through. I had no colours to help me as it wasn't the done thing to wear your colours back then, especially for a thirteen-year-old having to bus his way home on a Saturday afternoon.

'Bollocks, you ain't London with a voice like that.' Then I did the most stupid thing, I turned and ran as if to admit they were right. They chased me for all they were worth but they were never going to get near me, I was the one who was shitting himself. I had never set foot in a pub before in my life, but I burst through those doors like a rocket, shouting out for my Dad. The place was full and it took ages to find him, and in that time the tears started to flow down my face. Eventually I found him and blabbed out what had happened.

Dad's mates thought this was hysterical but he went mad. 'We ain't northerners. My son ain't a fucking northerner.' He dragged me out of the pub leaving his mates and, more surprisingly, his pint behind. 'Where are the little fuckers? I ain't having that, we're going to get this sorted. Little bastards.' To this day, I don't think I have ever seen him so angry.

We found the kids. Dad grabbed the leader by the hair, pushed him against the wall and in no uncertain terms explained that I was a Londoner and West Ham through and through. They got our full family history, even I found out things I never knew: his school, youth club, where his first girlfriend's dad's shop was, etc. It was starting to get embarrassing before he finally made them all apologise to me and shake my hand. The kids did get the chance to explain – the accent, no colours – and Dad seemed prepared to accept their mistake. As for me, I just stood there sniffling, humiliated and hungry.

Dad has been called The Northerner ever since by his mates, something he has never forgiven me for. He still won't accept that I was more than prepared to wash my own pants after that experience. I have never been so scared.

Dad made me go to the next few games after that, despite me wanting to stay at home, and looking back on it I am glad he did, because I might never have gone back. But I stuck to him like glue until a few years later when he stopped going himself after losing his job and having to change his career.

I still follow the Hammers and now take in more away games than home ones, as I still live up here – which poses its own problems, mainly convincing the police and stewards that I am not trying to infiltrate the away end in order to cause trouble. I won't wear the replica shirts or any colours, but carry a bobble hat which stays well-hidden in my pocket until the time is right to show my allegiance. On a few occasions the accent has even helped me out, but I guess it owes me one. The trouble is well on the decline now, but if you travel by car like I always do then you can find yourself in the odd dodgy situation. It's still there, and if the game is on Sky then I'll stay at home. Unlike most others, pay-per-view is something that I would welcome.

Football violence nearly killed this game and almost denied me some of the greatest moments of my life. West Ham have always had plenty of meatheads following them and that makes it harder for those who, like me, want nothing to do with it. It's us that get the odd slap in the town centre, car parks and back streets.

I don't understand it and never want to, but I know that it frightened the shit out of me. If it ever comes back then I'll follow the game from the comfort of my own armchair. The club has come a long way over the last few years, I only hope they can keep it up.

The first trip to the capital with the lads can be quite an experience, especially when you find you may just have stepped out of your depth. Mitch recalls his first big day out.

* * *

WHO ARE YA? . . . AND YOU? . . . AND YOU?

My one ambition is to go to the capital and really take it to the Cockneys, have just one real pop at one of the top firms. Us and them on their ground. I've had it away loads of times up here and elsewhere with them – some we won, some we didn't – but to go to the capital with the full mob would be something else. Like anyone involved in this, I have respect for all the lads at it, no matter what club they follow. It takes bollocks to get yourself up for it, especially when you think about the smaller mobs. That's something people on the outside can't understand, we have great respect for each other, a kind of common ground. I've tried to explain it to mates, but unless you have first-hand experience you won't get it, never.

I can't help but admire the Cockneys, I fucking hate them but I admire them. If you put the word out, they will show. They will come to you in numbers and front it. They ain't any harder than anyone else, far from it, not with firms like the Naughty Forty around, or the Zulu Army anyway, but they have the bottle all right. It's not a problem taking them on up here, but London is very different and I learnt that early on.

When I was seventeen we had the beginnings of a small firm coming together, all late teens or early twenties. We were doing all we could to make a name for ourselves and gain the respect of the main lads at the club. We had visited a few ends at away games, been on the edges of other more organised stuff, and had grown a bit cocky.

We had a game at Millwall and word was out that the main firm had something organised at Moorgate tube station for midday. We decided that it was time for the Cockneys to get a taste of what we had to offer and we wanted to be part of it. We knew that our mob would need all the numbers they could get and soon we were given the nod that we could be part of it.

They wouldn't all go down together as the police would

soon be onto them. The meeting point for us all was going to be Farringdon tube station. Most of the lads were driving down to Stanmore tube near the M1, getting the tube and changing at Wembley Park. Another lot were going to Edgware tube and changing at Euston. We made our own arrangements and decided to use British Rail into King's Cross rather than Euston, our usual stop, then the Metropolitan line to join everyone else.

It was our first trip to the capital as a mob and to be involved in something like this got the adrenaline going. On the day, we only got up to about eighteen in numbers as some of the lads had bottled it. As we were trying to build a reliable firm, they wouldn't be invited again, home or away. Some of the older lads had been telling us to watch our backs and be on the look-out at King's Cross for any spotters; after all, Millwall knew we were coming.

There was no drinking on the way down as we wanted to be on the case from the start and didn't want to fuck up, the plan being to drive down to St Albans and get the train in from there. We got off the train in twos and threes so that we wouldn't look like a mob, and had decided that we would check out the station before going down into the underground, each group going off to buy their tickets as we waited. There were plenty of lads around and every one looked like a potential Millwall fan.

I was standing by the burger place when these two blokes came over and stood next to us. The conversation went something like this.

'Are you football fans, because there is a massive off going on outside!'

'Is there? Who with?' I was genuinely interested.

'Come with me and I'll show you. It's you and half of London, mate.' He just looked at me and my mates as we stood there looking gob-smacked. 'If you think you're going to make it to Moorgate, you're dreaming.' With that, they walked off. As he went, he turned around, smiled and said, 'Chelsea, by the way. Be seeing ya.'

As I watched him join about ten other blokes, and I mean blokes, my legs went to jelly. They had placed themselves between us and the platform back to St Albans, forcing us either to go outside or, worse still, down the underground. I looked around for the other lads, not knowing whether to get them together or somehow let them know that we had been sussed out and they should try to get out before they were spotted.

We were well out of our league here and I just stood there not knowing what to do next. The other lads had sussed this out and didn't know what to do either, then one of them shouted for us to all get together. The Chelsea lot waited to see how many of us there were and we tried to make a move out of the station. Then the shout of 'Chelsea' went up and they came at us from everywhere, appearing from every doorway. We were well and truly fucked. Some of the lads did a runner and got chased out, the rest of us just laid down and took it before the police came steaming in to sort it out. Most of the Chelsea boys had vanished, but you could still see a few of the faces hanging around to see what plans the police had for us.

The police took us out of a side-entrance and lined us up against a wall. They had obviously been waiting for it to happen because there were five riot-vans ready and waiting, as well as the dog-handlers, and they weren't in the mood for fucking around. Some of our lot were missing and a few others that had managed to keep out of the way came over to join us. We had taken a good hiding and there was a lot of blood around. A few of the lads were mouthing off about the police letting us get turned over before they came in to sort it out, but we soon learnt that the London coppers don't fuck about. One of the lads was bundled into one of the vans and turned over before being thrown back to us. You know what it's like when you've had a hiding, you get past caring and he continued to mouth it. They had had enough by now, so they got him on the floor in front of us, put the cuffs on and gave him a few more digs before dragging him off screaming to the nick. That shut the rest of us up.

Then we got the talking-to from one of the coppers. We were told that if anyone else wanted to mouth off, his mates would be more than happy to escort them to the nick as well. Things had been going off all morning and apparently we had got off lightly. All the top London firms were out wanting a piece of the action: Chelsea and Spurs were all over the tube looking out for anyone they could find, and West Ham and the Millwall firm had already had it away at Liverpool Street. Some of the other group had been well turned-over at Euston and he told us there had been two stabbings. That really shit us up. We hadn't got to that stage yet, which was lucky because the coppers went through every pocket, but we knew the main mob had a few that would use a knife and the Cockneys were known for carrying blades. Farringdon tube had been closed off so there was no chance of knowing where the rest of the lads were. Then they gave us a choice of what we could do. We could either get back on the train to St Albans with a British Transport Police escort, get taken to Euston and put on the first train back north, or go down the tube and be left to look after ourselves, it was up to us. There was no way I was going down the underground.

Most of the lads decided that they had seen enough and would just go back home, but seven of us really wanted to make it to the game. We told the coppers what we wanted to do and asked them if we could get a taxi. They told us to wait while the others were taken back to the train. Once they had gone, they told us that they wouldn't let us make our own way down and were going to walk us up to Euston where some of the other lads were. They took us in through a side-door and onto a platform where about 60 lads were already waiting. They had been ambushed at Baker Street tube by some Millwall but given a good account of themselves. It was there that the stabbings had taken place; one of our lads had been slashed on the arm. It wasn't that bad, but they had taken him to hospital along with some other bloke – who he was they didn't know. The police obviously thought they had hold of the real hard-core and kept us waiting at the end of the platform, well out of the way. Loads of the lads were pissed-off, but others really wanted to get down to the game just to show they had the bottle. Then the police announced that they had two buses coming that would take us down to the game under escort. What a result, I had thought we were on the next train home.

We got down to the game about ten minutes late and the police had kept a small area away from everyone else up in the corner. Some other lads had made it down as well, but most had been stopped or given up. We were told that loads of the coaches had been bricked and that loads of people had been given slaps on the way to the ground. Everyone seemed pretty pissed off really, and the journey home was going to be a long one. After the end of the match, the police kept us back for ages and allowed some of the other lads, much to their relief, to join us. The coaches took us back to Euston, the police put us onto the train and British Transport Police stayed with us until Milton Keynes.

Now all that happened over twelve years ago, and I couldn't believe how organised the London firms were. It seemed they had people everywhere looking out for us. We stood no chance and things don't get any easier. You see, the problem we have is getting the numbers into town without everyone finding out. The tube is dangerous and I would never use it. Every stop is a potential ambush point and you never know who you will come up against. They know how to hit quickly and how to get out quickly, leaving us fucked. It is possible to take a small mob into town and do a quick hit, but you just can't arrange a real big off because people talk too easily and then you are taking on everyone and his mates as well as the coppers. That is exactly what happened with Birmingham and Stoke last year when they sorted things out with Millwall. Everyone up here knew what had been planned and that made the job easy for the police. It's a shame because they would both

have given Millwall a run for their money and it was something everyone wanted to happen. Everyone knows about
Millwall, they would have loved it and it would have been
good to see if they could have lived up to their reputation.
But if you think that Stoke and Brum weren't serious, then
you got it wrong.

PART TWO
Chelsea

Chapter 3
Flash, Brash And Dangerous

Of all the capital's clubs, there is one in particular that seems to epitomise that cockiness and one-upmanship which is an integral part of being a flash, cocky Londoner. That club is, of course, Chelsea. Even now, the club has that air of semi-sophisticated class about it that took it to such prominence back in the sixties and seventies, when the boys from the Bridge were *the* club to follow if you were, or aspired to be, a member of the trendy set. In the era of Osgood, Hudson and Cooke, Chelsea Football Club were as much a part of the King's Road and Carnaby Street movement as Mary Quant and Mick Jagger.

However, while the trendy set embraced Chelsea in a way that no other club has ever enjoyed since – and yes, that includes Man United – those fans who watched the game from the infamous 'Shed' were busy forging a reputation of their own. It quickly became obvious to us that we could have written a whole book about the Chelsea supporters, because they have a history of trouble dating back to the formation of the club itself. While this is something they have in common with most other clubs, Chelsea also have a number of unique features about the make-up of their support, which makes them worth a particularly close examination.

The real problems for Chelsea began in the sixties when the explosion of youth culture saw the birth of a number of movements such as the mods and the rockers who fought running battles at seaside resorts almost every Bank Holiday. When these movements began to decline in popularity (around 1966–67) they were replaced by a number of others, and one particular group, the skinheads, allied itself to Chelsea. This movement, originally born out of the ska and reggae music scene, was becoming synonymous with aggression and violence and found a very welcoming environment on the terraces at Stamford Bridge. The opportunity to fight with supporters of other London clubs had been a regular occurrence, but the availability of cheap travel, coupled with the relative affluence of West London, meant that the Chelsea faithful were able to take their reputation around the country, and they took to this with a passion.

Every Chelsea fixture became a potential battleground which the police forces of the country could barely contain. The reputation of the Chelsea supporters grew with almost every away match as they became possibly the most feared group of travelling fans in Britain, and with very good reason.

L*T*N

There'd been trouble almost everywhere and it had become a big part of the day out, it wasn't just about the football then. We'd gone up to L*t*n for a game and everyone had turned out, we'd been looking forward to this one. We were getting slaughtered on the pitch, the team were shit and we'd had enough. Once the match was lost we used to look to kick things off. The word went out that we were going to try and get the game stopped. About halfway through the second half, some of the lads got on the pitch and attacked their keeper, and things started to get a bit heavy with the police as they were determined to make sure that the game was finished. Afterwards, we went through the town like a fucking typhoon; windows, cars, the lot. Everything we could wreck, we wrecked. The coppers were run ragged; in the end they gave up and were nowhere to be seen. We ran riot.

We had totalled the town centre, and when we finally got to the station everyone was really buzzing because no one had been nicked or anything. We were doing whatever we wanted, and in those days you didn't have to worry about being filmed and pulled later. On the way back everyone started on the train, which was blitzed. It was totally mental; you had to be there to see what it was like, totally wrecked. When we got back into London the Old Bill just let us go, leaving them to clear up the mess. The railways stopped running football trains and made the clubs pay for the specials themselves after that. If you had seen the state it was in then you wouldn't blame them.

As the fortunes of the club, and so the support, declined, the resident hooligan element began to form a higher proportion of the club's following and in truth the majority of its travelling fans. The fear instilled by that travelling support has become legendary and it had the effect of attracting individuals who liked to be on the fringes of that violent culture.

During the mid-seventies, things began to take on a more sinister tone as members of Chelsea's violent following became openly linked with the far-right politics of the National Front. Their growth at this time was in no small way helped by its campaign to attract supporters from football clubs throughout the country. The party's desire to target angry, white young men as possible recruits led it directly to the football terraces, and there is no doubt that the NF was particularly successful in this respect at Stamford Bridge. The party's newspapers, the *Flag* and *Bulldog*, carried a 'league table' of sales at football grounds and were openly on sale in the Fulham Road before most home games. This table at least showed a highly successful Chelsea, as they were never out of the top four. Indeed, such was the influence of far-right politics at that time that many supporters actively refused to support black players wearing blue shirts, and those players were subjected to horrific racial abuse. We well remember a conversation with a group of individuals who refused to acknowledge goals scored by black players, even to the extent of constructing their own league table discounting those goals.

Following major trouble during the 1976–77 season, in particular at the final few matches, the Chelsea chairman at the time, Brian Mears, gave permission for fences to be erected at the Bridge and the place took on the appearance of a zoo. The unintended effect of this, far from deterring those intent on trouble, was to make the supporters behave like the animals they were thought to be. When they travelled to the grounds without the fences, things often became very ugly.

BIRMINGHAM

It was September 1980, both teams were going for promotion and Chelsea must have brought about 6,000 to St Andrews, every one of the fuckers chanting 'We are Nazis', giving the old salutes and all that shit. Birmingham hammered them 5–1, but just after we went 4–1 up they went fucking berserk. They came charging across the corner of the pitch and along the Spion Kop. We hadn't seen a mob like that before up here; our lot took one look and they were off! Well, me and my mate were about to leg it when we saw this woman of about thirty and her little lad, standing in the open space that was left. She was just stood there like she was in shock. Her lad was screaming and crying but she wasn't at home at all, and they were right in their path. Well, there was no way I could leave the poor cow there. We moved across to try and snap her out of it, or at least get the lad.

I tell you, I honestly thought we were in for a right pasting. The Chelsea lads came running forward and we were right in their path. It was like the parting of the Red Sea, they went right around us! I couldn't believe my luck, still can't. I really thought I was going to die. I doubt she or her lad ever went to football again.

The strange thing is, about a year after that, Birmingham fans really started to get themselves organised for the first time. That Chelsea mob were the catalyst for that, I'm absolutely certain.

That same month, the Chelsea fans came up against the ultimate challenge to their reputation. West Ham supporters fought running battles with them at Stamford Bridge as the East Enders tried their luck at taking the Shed. This battle resulted in 42 arrests and a definite boot up the arse for Chelsea as far as the opposition were concerned.

THE CLARETS AND THE BLUES

Chelsea were getting all the headlines then. Their fans were the most feared in the country and they were *the* London club as far as the press were concerned. Were they fuck! These blokes weren't Londoners, they came from Hertfordshire, Surrey and all that. We'd had enough of all that bollocks and this time we'd show them what London was. I don't mind admitting it but I wore a blue shirt that day. I've still got it at home and it's one of my greatest bits of memorabilia. We all had Chelsea shirts on and went up the Shed. They're all giving it the mouth, knowing they ain't going to get near our lads, and then we kicked it off. They couldn't make out why us lads in Chelsea shirts were laying into them, but they ran away. They had their lads and I got a few kicks once they sussed us out. Once we were on the pitch, the shirts came off and claret-and-blue was on underneath. They were going mental, but we took it to them and they knew they weren't top dogs any more. They would have to come to us now to win that back.

Chelsea were indeed a dangerous club to support. Everyone else was out to prove that they were the top dogs and the Chelsea lads were more than up for the challenge both at home and away. It was not until some Chelsea fans went on the rampage at Derby in November 1981 that the FA finally took action and ordered that all Chelsea away fixtures be made all-ticket. While the police endorsed this, the club decided to take the matter to the High Court and in February 1982, this ruling was lifted.

Chelsea's travelling fans seemed to make a point of turning over every ground they visited that hadn't yet been conquered, their reputation being enhanced almost week-by-week by the sheer numbers of active hooligans following the club. You knew that if Chelsea were coming to town, so were up to a few thousand hooligans and if you were a club who were at it, then this fixture in particular, home or away, would be your biggest test. At the time, Chelsea had three clubs outside London with which they had particularly fierce rivalries: Manchester United, due almost entirely to battles with the infamous 'Cockney Reds' during away trips; Leicester City, as a result of Chelsea taking over the town, the home end and almost everything else in 1980 and again in 1981, followed by City's attempts to even the score (!); and most famous of all, Leeds United.

The rivalry with Leeds actually dates back to before the 1970 FA Cup final, but primarily revolves around the fact that Don Revie's side of that era were massively unpopular, very successful and enjoyed a decidedly volatile following of their own. Certainly Leeds were one of the few clubs who had the numbers to come to the capital without the normal fears and were more than capable of putting on a show. The main factor in this rivalry was that while Chelsea were the archetypal London club, all money and flash, Leeds epitomised Yorkshire and the North, which to the average southerner meant flat caps, whippets and *Coronation Street*. The two sets of fans have nothing but loathing for each other, something which has spilled over into violence on many occasions, as this Leeds fan was only too happy to tell us:

LEEDS

At the beginning of the eighties, the Leeds United firm were notorious, the top firm in the country no matter what any Cockney bastard tells you. We were named the 'Leeds Service Crew', after the early-morning trains we took to away games, and were at it until about 1988 when the police finally broke it all up with the undercover Operation Wild Boar. In truth, the firm was staring to split anyway as loads of the lads were getting into the acid-house scene. Dance music, acid and pills were the new buzz then.

Well, we'd always had a rivalry with Chelsea and always took numbers down there to put on a show, because there was no way we could take a running from them after everything that's gone on over the years. Anyway, we took about 150 down, real head-cases they were in those days, and arrived at Euston about midday. There wasn't a copper in sight, so we got onto the tube and headed down to Piccadilly Circus, where we came across the sight of about 200 Chelsea boys waiting on the westbound platform. They hadn't clocked us at all and it was mayhem and chaos down there. The Chelsea boys were taken completely by surprise because we got to them almost before they knew what was happening. We kicked the fuck out of them, absolutely battered them. For them it was backs-to-the-wall stuff and they couldn't get out of there quick enough, Cockney shit. After about ten minutes the Old Bill came steaming in so we turned on them as well. We owed those Met bastards one and they were getting it in numbers. We attacked the police with scaffolding and bricks from some renovation work on the platform. Eventually, the police got on top of us and trapped us on the platform. But we whipped their arses down there.

After about half an hour of the game, we began the old 'When I was just a little boy . . .' chant and the Chelsea fans above us started spitting down on us and giving us loads of verbal. The Leeds then started breaking up the seating and the fences, using the stuff as missiles aimed at the police on the touchline. We had a right time of it. There were smoke-bombs going off and the game ended about 25 minutes late. There were over 200 arrests that day and we showed those fuckers Leeds run from no one. We took it to them and ran them ragged all day.

* * *

Unlike West Ham and Millwall – and to a lesser extent their North London rivals – whose supporters traditionally come from the local area, the core of the Chelsea support has always seemingly existed in the suburbs. Many of the most violent and feared groups came from the western outskirts of London such as Greenford, and those of us who travelled into London on match days had more chance of meeting groups of Chelsea fans than those of any other club. The tube network was at times the place of which nightmares are made, as Paul S. from Ealing relates.

FULHAM BROADWAY TUBE

We'd been to the Bridge to see Chelsea play Derby and after the game, were waiting at Fulham Broadway station which was, as usual, rammed with Chelsea fans. In those days, it wasn't a good idea to get too close to the edge of the platform because when a train was coming in, some twat would start a push and more than one bloke almost ended up under a train. Well, somehow this Derby fan had found himself on the platform and the Chelsea fans had given him a right hiding. It didn't matter what you looked like or anything, if you wasn't wearing blue you were fair game and in them days Chelsea didn't fuck about. Anyway, he was on the floor when the train starts to pull in. I have never been so frightened in all my life, I honestly thought I was going to see someone get murdered. These two lads grabbed this poor Derby bloke off the floor – I mean, this lad had taken such a beating that he was like a rag doll – they then swung him out in front of the tube train before pulling him back just in time. Fuck me, this guy screamed like I've never heard before; it was frightening, a really horrible noise. The driver's face was scary, I am sure he thought that was it as well. These Chelsea lads thought this was hysterical and just dropped him on the platform and got on the train.

This lad was crying his eyes out, but all the Chelsea lads on the train were laughing and taking the piss. I stayed on the platform, as did a few others. This poor sod needed help as he was in real shock. Whenever I go on the tube after a match, I always think it could happen again. It gets so packed down there.

While the average Chelsea 'geezer' was one thing, the early eighties again saw the right-wing element of the support begin to grow in number. As the influence of the National Front and British Movement began to wane at other clubs, those who had been attracted more by the politics than the football started to see Stamford Bridge as their unofficial headquarters. This continued to bring severe problems to the club, as the media were now all over them. The new chairman, Ken Bates, purposefully set out to remove the right-wing support, which he blamed almost totally for the club's terrible reputation. In August 1982, the board took the step of writing to the club's supporters to condemn the racists who followed Chelsea and informed them in no uncertain terms that their actions would only spur the club on to attract more black players and supporters. However, this had the effect of boosting their already infamous reputation and initially had no real effect on their activities.

Chelsea supporters continued to be active on the hooligan front within the domestic game, but now also began to play a major role in trouble involving England fans on their travels. At almost every incident involving supporters of the national side, and they were regular occurrences, followers of Chelsea were implicated. In 1982 they played probably the most active role so far during England's World Cup campaign in Spain. It was reported in a number of British newspapers at the time that Chelsea supporters constituted the premier focus for National Front activity at football and that a large majority of those fans were present in Spain. Amazingly, the British press were for once correct in their reporting. It was clear to many of the England fans in Spain at the time that a group of Chelsea supporters sharing right-wing beliefs were there to put on a show of force and to recruit. It has to be said, too, that with the Falklands War still raging, they were not unsuccessful.

The trouble at the '82 World Cup was intense and was, to a

large extent, politically motivated and orchestrated by the right-wing element. The Falklands conflict and the ongoing situation in Gibraltar caused a great deal of anti-British sentiment in Spain, and this was food and drink to the National Front groups, among whom Chelsea supporters were the driving force.

SPAIN '82

Looking back on it now, it was all a bit pathetic. But the thing in Spain was that the police were really heavy and if you stuck close to the Chelsea lads, you were pretty safe because they would always back you up.

I remember after the French game, we were in a bar and there were loads of Froggies running around outside and a couple of English lads got a slap. The Chelsea lads were there like a fucking shot, kicked the shit out of these French bastards and rescued these English lads. Fair play to them, if you're in trouble with England you can almost always rely on Chelsea. The Front boys were a bit of a pain though, really in-your-face all the time as if it was your duty to join up with them. It was all new to me and the lads back then. Politics was something your old man was interested in.

The thing was, plenty of us younger lads fell for it, what with the Falklands and that, and a few from our club ended up getting involved in all that shit. Being with these lads made you feel safe, though. That was part of the draw as well, I think, with it being our first time abroad with England and everything. The NF lads weren't all there for the football, though. There was loads of shit going on, meetings with Basque groups and things like that. That wasn't about football. All that 'there ain't no black in the Union Jack' stuff, that's bollocks.

Back on the domestic front, Chelsea and their supporters were still very active on the hooligan scene. At Brighton on the second Saturday of the 1983–84 season, they went on the rampage and fought running battles with Brighton fans during which seven policemen were injured. Despite this, the FA took no action and the supporters continued to cause problems wherever they went, right through 1983 and into 1984.

At Southampton on 20 October 1984, Chelsea supporters fought running battles with police and Southampton fans in an incident that was to become known locally as the 'Battle of Hill Lane'. There had been minor incidents throughout the town prior to the game and also in the ground, but it was afterwards that things turned really nasty. As the Chelsea fans were being escorted from the ground, a large number had escaped the police lines and vanished into sidestreets in an attempt to get back towards the Southampton fans, who themselves were trying to get within missile-range of Chelsea. As the main group passed Springhill Roman Catholic Primary School, dozens of Chelsea supporters jumped the fence and some found their way onto the roof of the school buildings. As the police went in to drive them out, they began smashing windows, overturning playground furniture and breaking down fencing, which they then used as weapons against the police. This attack was followed by a hail of coins and then bricks as garden walls were kicked over and dismantled. Police in riot gear were deployed, for the first time ever in Southampton, in order to drive them out of Hill Lane and down to the central station. For the Chelsea fans, this was merely the start and the return journey to London saw a number of serious incidents. In Basingstoke, a coach-load of Chelsea fans fought with local youths and smashed numerous windows after being refused entry to a nightclub while in Hayling Island, a mob of 150 Chelsea battled with locals in a pub, where a barman was also stabbed in the head with a meat-skewer.

Chelsea continued to enhance their already-bad reputation wherever they travelled and in early 1985 they were drawn to play Sunderland over two legs in the Milk Cup semi-final, a couple of fixtures that were to leave yet another black mark on the history of Chelsea FC.

With the first leg at Roker Park and a Wembley appearance on the horizon, Chelsea supporters headed for the north-east in their thousands and trouble started almost as soon as they began arriving. In Bishop Auckland, some 25 miles from Sunderland, a coach-load of supporters stopped for a pre-match drink that resulted in a number of offs with local youths, while in Sunderland itself, approximately 30 Chelsea fans fought with locals and police on the seafront. During the actual match, there were numerous incidents as Chelsea fans infiltrated all areas of the ground. With the police at full stretch, at least three officers were injured as they attempted to get into the crowd to arrest Chelsea fans who were causing trouble. With the Blues losing 2–0, their supporters began ripping up seats and hurling them at the home fans. The trouble continued after the game, with Chelsea supporters intent on causing maximum disruption in the sure-fire knowledge that the return leg would see Sunderland bring a committed firm down to take them on. A good example of this was clearly seen an hour after the match, when a bus-load of Chelsea turned up at a pub full of Sunderland supporters, kicked their way past the doormen and blitzed the place, attacking customers, throwing bottles and glasses, and then vanishing before the police could arrive. In all, 91 supporters were arrested that night and it was clear that the return leg, with so much at stake, would be even worse.

SUNDERLAND

We were expecting them to come down in numbers. After all, this was a big game with Wembley as the prize. They were sure to have a firm, especially after what happened at their place, and as usual all the Chelsea were out.

Before the game, we'd had it away on the underground but it wasn't their main lads, I am sure. When Speedie scored to get us back in the tie, the atmosphere was excellent – but Clive Walker shouldn't ever show his face around here again after what he did to his old club, the bastard. When he scored the second goal for them, loads of Chelsea got onto the pitch wanting to get the game abandoned, and some lads were after their players. After a couple of minutes, the police brought the horses in and they were running about like idiots while the ref took all the players into the centre of the pitch. But that was pretty useless because the supporters were lobbing anything they could at the police: bottles, seats, the fucking lot. One bloke then got through the police and went to have a go at Clive Walker and the Chelsea players had to drag him off, which was a bit out of order really as that cunt had just knocked us out of the Cup. They got the game started again and, near the end, Speedie got sent off, which started it all up again; but by then the coppers were all over us. This one geezer got arrested and cuffed in the ground. His mates turned the police over and he got away, but they couldn't get the cuffs off so he was fucked.

Anyway, outside the ground it was mental. Sunderland were really giving it the biggie because they had got to Wembley. We were going fucking mental.

On the night of the Sunderland game, West Ham had been playing Wimbledon in an FA Cup fifth round tie and a number of Hammers supporters had headed up to Stamford Bridge for a supposedly pre-arranged 'off' with both Chelsea and Sunderland. The Sunderland mob, having been all but slaughtered by Chelsea, quickly left the area and now West Ham took on their rivals in a number of fierce exchanges in the streets around the ground. The worst incident took place when a train full of almost 600 West Ham fans made an unscheduled extended stop at Parsons Green tube station after the communication cord was pulled. The train had come to a stop next to a platform full of Chelsea, who then attacked the train in an effort to get at the West Ham fans – who were at the same time attempting to get out at Chelsea. The guards, realising what was about to happen, refused to open the doors, but the Chelsea supporters then began smashing the windows with seats off the platform, stones off the track and a stretcher from the first-aid post. The Chelsea fans then began climbing onto the train in an effort to get at their rivals, while the West Ham were climbing off to get at those on the platform and a major confrontation took place. When the train eventually pulled out of the station, a number of Chelsea supporters actually ran after it along the track.

In all, over 20 policemen were injured and over 100 supporters arrested in incidents surrounding that game, and there is no doubt that this was a turning point for the club. Ken Bates decided, yet again, that enough was enough. He was determined to deal with the hooligan element once and for all, and with the FA certain to take stern action against the club following the Sunderland game, he went on the offensive. He initially threatened to close the East Stand, which was where the trouble had started, but then came up with probably the most novel idea ever tried in the battle against hooliganism. In a season that also saw Millwall fans riot at L*t*n, two Chelsea fans jailed following incidents surrounding the Manchester United fixture in December 1984 (one for life, the other for eight years) and 25 members of the Cambridge United firm, the 'Pringle Mob', jailed for a vicious attack which, ironically, left 40 innocent Chelsea fans seriously injured, Mr Bates felt that drastic measures were the only option left. He was convinced that the only way to deal with the trouble-makers was to wire up the Stamford Bridge fence to the mains, thereby electrocuting anyone who went near it and at least preventing pitch invasions! Despite his best intentions, the move was greeted with uproar by the supporters and horror by the Greater London Council (GLC), who took the club to court to prevent its use. Bates stood firm, but in the end realised that legally he was on very dodgy ground and the fence was never switched on. However, he had sent a strong message to the club's supporters, and in the aftermath of the tragic events that unfolded in the final weeks of the season – Bradford, the death of a supporter at the Birmingham–Leeds fixture, Heysel and the banning of English clubs from Europe – things finally began to calm down. Following these major incidents, large-scale riots became a thing of the past almost overnight.

With the game under ever-increasing scrutiny from the government, the police were given a new role to play. Their goal was to smash the organised football firms, of which Chelsea were seen as one of the biggest. In May 1986, five alleged ringleaders of

Chelsea's notorious gang, the Headhunters, were jailed for a total of 28 years, sending another clear message, not just to Chelsea supporters but to hooligans throughout the country, that their day had been and gone. The clubs, who had aspirations of returning to the European scene, were also under pressure to deal with their own hooligans and began to install closed-circuit television (CCTV), regarded by the police, and many supporters, as the best weapon of all.

While to a large extent this move was a success, the good work accomplished by a great many individuals at Stamford Bridge was always in danger of being undone and that is exactly what happened at the end of the 1987–88 season. Facing Middlesbrough in a play-off over two legs with their First Division status on the line, Chelsea could only manage a 1–0 victory in the second leg at Stamford Bridge, lost 2–1 on aggregate and were relegated. As the final whistle blew, hundreds of Boro fans spilled onto the track behind the goal at their end to celebrate. A huge mob of Chelsea supporters then charged onto the pitch, attacking Boro fans, ambulancemen and policemen, with the result that 102 supporters were arrested. The FA, with the 1988 European Championships in Germany a matter of weeks away, were furious. Although the threatened removal of England from the championships did not take place, Chelsea were hit with a £75,000 fine, had their terraces closed for five games and were given a severe warning by the FA.

The following season in the Second Division was a good one both for Chelsea on the pitch (they went up as champions) and their hooligan following on the terraces. New grounds and new foes meant that on their travels they were as active as ever, but their next major appearance on the back pages was not to be until 25 March 1990, when they appeared at Wembley in the final of the Zenith Data Systems Cup against, of all people, Middlesbrough. For the Boro fans, the memories of 1988 were still fairly fresh and they brought a massive contingent to London for the final, many of whom were not only expecting trouble but actually looking for it.

* * *

DOWN THE WEST END

We knew the Boro would head for the West End and we wanted to have a serious pop at them before heading up to Wembley. We initially waited at King's Cross, but when the Old Bill turned up in numbers we headed down to Trafalgar Square. The police tried to keep hold of us, but with so many tourists around it's easy to give them the shake.

We spotted a group of about ten Boro fans come up out of Leicester Square tube and head up towards Covent Garden. We were on our way after them when they turned down this side alley. We went to go straight down but they had obviously sussed us and as we turned in, they were right there with the Stanley knives out. I don't need cutting up, so we left them to it. They didn't come after us, but if you carry a knife then you're going to use it.

In all, there were 46 arrests before the game and another 22 afterwards as trouble continued all over North London until late evening.

Following the Zenith Data Systems final, many of the Chelsea supporters turned their thoughts to the summer months, and it was clear that Chelsea supporters were again a dominant force among the hooligan groups who travelled to the World Cup in Italy. Following England's defeat in the semi-final against Germany in Turin, Chelsea fans were alleged to have thrown flaming bottles of paint-stripper mixed with petrol at Italian locals, as well as being implicated in the earlier events in Cagliari and Rimini.

On the domestic front, the violence inside grounds had apparently calmed down for good, primarily as a result of the tragedy at Hillsborough in 1989. Supporters began to realise that things had gone too far, and the subsequent Taylor Report made sure that the grounds at least would now become as safe as they possibly could. (Thankfully, it was to be another two years before a serious incident took place inside a ground, and that was outside the top division. It happened at St Andrews when Birmingham and Stoke City ran riot in February 1992.)

The formation of the Premier League was the next significant step, and with football being marketed to a whole new audience, the hooligan groups took their activities onto a new and more organised level. The use of mobile phones to plan meetings with rival firms became the norm, while the media, almost certainly driven by the desperate need to fill the back pages with good news and so not upset the fledgling Premier League, took the decision to stop reporting on trouble around stadia.

This did not deter the Chelsea hooligans and they continued to fight their way around the country. However, it was not until 1995 that they forced their way back into the headlines, and they did so with a vengeance.

The year had begun badly with the Eric Cantona incident at Selhurst Park – something even the great British press could not ignore – but in the same week, Chelsea travelled to the New Den for an FA Cup tie, a fixture guaranteed to cause nightmares for the Metropolitan Police.

As expected, there was a great deal of trouble at the match and it was the Chelsea fans who were largely to blame. While there had already been trouble outside the ground, inside the New Den it quickly became clear that Chelsea had infiltrated certain sections of the stadium and were intent on turning Millwall over. Despite a number of minor incidents in the first half, it was not until the second half got underway that things began to get really nasty.

MILLWALL

We had got ten tickets in the side stands for the game and had decided earlier in the day that we would wait until the first goal before we made it clear we were Chelsea. Once it became clear that we were playing shit and might lose, we thought we might as well go for it just after half-time. The natives were starting to suss us out as it was, anyway. It had already been going off since the start in other parts of the ground and there had even been an off right in front of us, but we had kept out of it.

Anyway, about five minutes into the second half we went for it. There was just this mass movement away from us then loads of their boys come steaming in, but we stood our ground and did all right. The coppers got us pretty quick and threw us in with the rest of our lads. About four minutes from the end, we steamed their mob next to us and it really kicked off big style, I mean about ten minutes' serious rowing. I got hit with something and went down. They were lobbing seats and coins at us – a typical wanky Millwall trick, that – and I ended up with the ambulance boys.

In all, it had taken 12 mounted policemen and 200 officers and stewards to keep the mobs apart. The police came under attack from around 50 Millwall fans who were determined to get back at the Chelsea supporters, and three officers were admitted to hospital. Following the drawn match, the replay was sure to be as hot-blooded – and so it proved.

The police had swamped the area for the replay, determined to ensure that the events of the previous week would not be repeated, and to be fair, they were pretty successful before the game began. With so much at stake, the atmosphere was electric. As the game progressed, Mark Stein scored for Chelsea and that seemed to calm the aggression among their supporters, but when Millwall equalised, some of their fans came onto the pitch to celebrate and had to be quickly removed by stewards.

Seeing visiting fans on your pitch is something that can stir even the most mild fan, and the Chelsea supporters were certainly becoming restless. While an attempted pitch-invasion was averted by police and stewards, things went from bad to worse when the game went through extra-time and ended with a penalty shoot-out. When John Spencer missed to ensure a Millwall victory the Chelsea supporters invaded the pitch from the North Stand, and two Millwall players were attacked. Mounted police managed to keep them away from the Millwall enclosure, but supporters from both ends now began ripping up seats and throwing them onto the pitch. While actual large-scale violence was avoided inside the ground, outside things were completely different as supporters fought running battles, hurling bottles and bricks at each other. CS gas was also used, primarily by Millwall supporters, against the police, leaving 20 of them injured, and 33 fans were arrested.

Ken Bates heaped the blame on a certain section of known Chelsea supporters, as did the press, and it was clear that the home fans were indeed the main culprits. Calls for a return to fencing at Stamford Bridge were made by numerous ill-informed people from within the game, but eventually common sense prevailed. However, the fact that the game had been televised and the scenes were being replayed with alarming frequency did not help matters, and the following months were to see further indications that the hooligans were intent on a resurgence.

Only a week after the Stamford Bridge riot, Chelsea fans, and in particular the Headhunters, were being held up as the main instigators of the violent scenes that surrounded England's fixture with Ireland in Dublin. Before the dust had settled on that one, Chelsea had yet another problem on their hands when the club travelled to Belgium for a European Cup-Winners' Cup tie against Bruges. Advance claims by the Belgian authorities that Chelsea fans were up there with the worst in Europe hardly helped matters, nor did warnings that right-wing groups from Britain, Belgium, Germany, France and Holland would also be active at the game. With these warnings ringing in their ears, the Belgian police set out on a massive anti-hooligan exercise.

BRUGES

We had booked our trip with a company we had used before on both Chelsea and England tours, so we didn't expect any problems and after catching the coach in London and travelling to Belgium via the ferry, we arrived in Bruges the night before the match. After settling into the hotel, a group of around twelve of us set off to hit the town and enjoy some good food and drink. There were plenty of Chelsea around, many pissed-up on the Belgian beer but most just having a laugh, really. We knew that many of the Chelsea heavies were in town and stories of the odd off were doing the rounds. Apparently, the local constabulary were none too impressed with what had landed on their doorstep. Bruges is a lovely city, and the sight of loads of drunken Chelsea fans in the main streets, shouting, pissing up walls and being sick, took the edge off it for most of us; and the sight of the riot police outside any bar where an Englishman was spotted saw us return to our hotel early on and finish our drinking off there.

In the morning, our courier told us that the police had decided to issue vouchers to the tour companies, which were to be traded for match tickets on the day. This was done, we were told, to avoid tickets getting onto the black market, and he was now off to the police station to collect our match tickets and would be back at the hotel for midday; we could collect our tickets then. So off we went for a morning's sightseeing.

When we returned at around one o'clock, we found about 20 of our group standing outside the hotel going mental. Apparently, when our courier had gone to the police station, the police had just taken the vouchers and told him to fuck off – and that was exactly what he had done! After telephoning the hotel to let them know, he had decided that, rather than face around 50 very unhappy Chelsea fans, he should catch the train back to the port and return to Blighty, leaving the hotel manager and the coach driver to deal with the situation. Cheers, mate!

Once the initial shock and anger had died down, there was only one thing we could do: go back into the centre and try and find a tout. We would sort out the tour company when we returned. There were hundreds of Chelsea around by now and loads were looking for tickets. One group had told us not to worry as the police always opened a section for those without tickets rather than leave them out on the streets playing up. I had seen this happen before myself but didn't want to risk it, so our search continued. We split up into smaller groups to make things easier and agreed to meet at the ground at around six o'clock, to find out how we had all got on. To our amazement, we found a bar within an hour where the barman said he could get us sixteen tickets, all for the Chelsea end! We gave him the money and he went off to make a phone call. Now I've seen loads of trouble following Chelsea and would rather avoid it if possible. Only very rarely have I ever got involved and that's always been when someone has started on me, because I go for the football. But we were really worried about getting into the game and were pretty pissed-off with what had happened to us, and with this in mind, we decided that if he didn't come with the tickets within an hour we would turn his bar over. Five minutes later he came back and said the tickets were on their way. Twenty minutes later they arrived. In one stroke he became our best friend and we became the best customers he could have hoped for. Although we were relieved, you could tell that all the lads felt they had paid for the same ticket twice, and that someone had taken a back-hander somewhere along the line.

News was coming back that the locals were now on the lookout for trouble and being backed up by the police when any Chelsea fans retaliated. Of course, you never get to hear this stuff back home, because what the press want to report is that Chelsea were on the rampage. The way things were going, it looked like they might get what they wanted, so we decided to make our way to the ground.

Once we arrived, we checked our tickets were kosher and hung around. The police were well kitted-out and seemed quite keen on the prospect of whacking the odd Englishman. I saw loads of lads, just pissed-up and singing, getting shoved about and having the horses pushing into them. The police had the batons out and were waving them about, and the whole atmosphere had become very intimidating just because the Old Bill wanted to put on a show.

We met up with the rest of the lads. Some had got tickets, but not all for the Chelsea end; others were in panic. They had met with other fans turned over by the police for tickets as we had been, and heard that a small group of Chelsea had been beaten up in a bar by the local boys. They had also seen Chelsea fans fighting and told us that things were being organised for after the match. Chelsea have always had a certain element that cause trouble, everyone knows that, and at away games you see faces you never get down the Bridge. At big away games you see faces you haven't seen in years; and in Europe you see faces of people you thought had died years ago, and for this game they were out in force. The police were constantly giving them the come-on, but these lads know the rules only too well. Despite the intimidation, they didn't bite and the game, from where I was standing, went off without a problem.

When we left the stadium, most of the Chelsea wanted to return to the centre. The police wanted to keep us together whether we wanted to go into town or not, but many of the hard-core tried to break off into smaller groups in order to lose the police and move undetected. This caused a few scuffles, so we stayed with the main group to avoid any trouble. As we got into the centre you could tell that loads had broken away. The police had also reduced in numbers.

When we got to the centre, the police sort of allocated us a few bars to drink in, so we decided to stay and have a few drinks, hoping the tension would die down, and then we would go to another, quieter part of the town. Police lined up on the other side of the road, watching our every move. Anyone trying to leave was stopped, questioned and sent back to the bar. They were being well over the top. If you did that to a foreign supporter over here you would get shot. The atmosphere in the bar was becoming more hostile and all we could do was drink, as when you went outside, it was clear that it was only a matter of time before the trouble would start. It was obvious that things were going off elsewhere. Sirens were blaring out and the police were becoming agitated; every now and then they would huddle together, listening to their radios. Some of the known

Chelsea boys looked like they had decided the time had come to try another bar. We were sure this was going to kick it off, because I knew the police would have none of it and so did the Chelsea lads.

I decided to move in the other direction, as I thought the police would wade into those trying to leave at the end of the street; it was 'look after number one' time. Sure enough, the police charged across to block off the road and a few lads started to make a dash for it while others stood their ground. The police just steamed in and let them have it, no questions, and started to batter anyone they could. The vans then shot forward and some of the Chelsea left in the bar came out throwing bottles and glasses at the police. Lads were getting hit on the head and kicked on the floor as the police made arrest after arrest, but some were giving as good back. A policeman came at me, waving his truncheon above my head. All I could do was duck down, protect my head with my arms and run back into the bar. I was waiting for that truncheon to come down on me, but thankfully it never did.

All those left had regrouped and some were ready to have a go at the police. I remember thinking they were mad – the police had helmets, batons, shields, God knows what, but what scared me most was the fact that these lads really meant it. Some of our group had got away, but one had been whacked across the legs just above the knee. All I wanted to do was get back to my hotel and then home. Across the road, TV crews and photographers had appeared and were taking pictures, and this was really making some Chelsea angry. The photographers would be as much of a target as the police if it went off again. I really wanted to get out of there. The bar owner obviously wanted us out, he must have been shitting himself – I was. Loads of the lads were just helping themselves to the beer, not just to drink but also wanting the bottles to throw. I think the police had over-looked the fact that the bar was acting as a constant supply of weapons. After about 20 minutes of calm, the police also decided they wanted us out and they lined up opposite. Some of the main lads were fronting it up when, over a loud-hailer, the police announced that we would be allowed to leave in small groups and return to our hotels.

Most of those trapped in the bar couldn't wait to get out, as they were like me. But I must say that I was glad the top lads were around, because I am sure they made the police worried and kept them from battering the shit out of loads of innocent people. I know our lads like to play up, but this was all down to the local police. They had treated us like animals and looked like they were enjoying themselves at the same time. We made sure that we were one of the first groups to be allowed to leave. As we went through the police lines, the photographers were taking our photos. It's funny, but most of us covered our faces to avoid being identified. It wasn't until my mate shouted to them that they should be photographing the police rather than us that I realised what I was doing: I was making myself look guilty. I said to my mate that we would probably appear on the front pages tomorrow, and I actually became worried that we would. Thankfully we didn't, but the good old English press made sure that a few did. Mostly they were of lads being led away in handcuffs or having their faces rammed into the tarmac with three police on their back. That only tells half the story; you had to be there to get the truth.

As for the tour company – well, the poor sod had left and unless the government step in, the company can do fuck all as their hands are tied. Still we're only football fans, we deserve it.

In all, the Belgian police refused entry to over 500 fans, rounded up and deported almost a thousand and arrested 354. They then remarked that it was 'as near to war as you can get without bullets'. The warnings about right-wing groups proved to be true and a calling card from the Dutch firm, the Utrecht Headhunters, was found in the city centre, as were three known German extremists who were arrested before the game. The Belgian fans were also intent on having a go at Chelsea to enhance their own reputation, and the feared Bruges mob, the East-siders, were joined outside the ground after the match by other groups of well-known Belgian firms from Ghent and Antwerp and had to be dispersed with water cannon. However, it was clear that in the hooligan stakes, Chelsea had indeed 'done the business' in Bruges.

Back home, the government, FA and media were incensed. Coming so soon after Millwall and Dublin, and with Euro 96 on the horizon, the activities of the Chelsea fans were the last thing anyone needed, but of more immediate concern was the fact that Chelsea had made it through to the next round in Europe and were due to play Zaragoza in Spain just one month later.

The FA went on the offensive, pleading with the Spanish club not to sell tickets to anyone other than their own supporters. Chelsea, well aware that they were under intense scrutiny, strictly monitored their own allocation to ensure that known trouble-makers did not get any tickets from the club. (This was done not only in the hope that they would not then travel, but also so that in the event of trouble, the club could distance itself from the hooligan element.) However, this did not deter many hundreds of ticketless Chelsea fans from travelling and huge numbers made their way to Spain to find tickets freely on sale at the ground. What they also found on their arrival was a police force intent on suppressing anything remotely like a football riot by using any means at its disposal. The feeling was that it was the attitude of the Spanish police that caused many of the problems at this game, the mere fact that you were English was enough to qualify you for a whack with a baton. By the time the game began, the mood among many Chelsea fans was one of outright hatred for the Spanish. Once the team conceded a third goal, effectively ending their European campaign, things began to get ugly and repeated baton-charges by the police left 12 supporters injured. This led to Chelsea supporters ripping up seats and using them as missiles, which in turn led to more baton charges and yet more injuries.

Outside the ground, things were even worse; the police, now warming to their task, made repeated charges at the Chelsea supporters, who by now could not wait to get out of the country.

Upon their arrival back in England, the media were all over the Chelsea fans once again, attacking them for their behaviour, but it quickly became apparent that on this occasion the mood was a very different one. The usual cocky attitude of returning English supporters had been replaced by one of anger and resentment. People returning with broken limbs and bandaged heads provoked fury among many supporters throughout the country, yet neither the government nor the FA protested or acted in any way to extract either an apology or recompense.

For the FA, concerns about Euro 96 were paramount. When the tournament did get underway, Chelsea fans were once again involved in trouble, as were fans from all over the country. Certainly, the West End of London saw a number of incidents involving Chelsea supporters – including the initial 'off' at the Porcupine pub near Leicester Square, which was the catalyst for the attack on the Scots in Trafalgar Square – but overall, Chelsea fans played a quieter role than expected during the tournament. Such is their reputation that many of the so-called 'lesser' clubs from around the country were looking to the Chelsea mobs to take the lead, but they made it known that they had no intention of becoming involved with any other club. The reasons for this are difficult to fathom, but the inference that no one is good enough to run with Chelsea is probably as good a reason as any.

Following Euro 96, and with the English game on a high, Chelsea entered the 1996–97 season on a note of extreme optimism. The Ruud Gullit era was underway and the influx of foreign stars to the first-team squad made a mockery of the right-wing following historically associated with the club. Even the supporters were behaving themselves, but everything was shattered by the death of the fans' favourite director, Matthew Harding, in a helicopter crash. While this in itself was bad enough, one of the consequences of his tragic death was that opposing fans began using it as a method of winding up the Chelsea faithful. This was first seen at Nottingham Forest in January 1997 and caused massive anger among those in the ground, resulting in violence outside following the final whistle.

Football fans have long memories and this certainly touched a raw nerve with the Chelsea fans. Time will tell if other clubs will adopt this theme, but hopefully they will not. The bottom line, though, is that over the years, Chelsea supporters have become synonymous with football violence and right-wing politics and this is a tag that the club will always struggle to remove. It has to be said, however, that for many among their paying and travelling hordes, it is a tag they are happy to carry.

Chapter 4
The Headhunters

Chelsea are known to have a number of smaller mobs rather than a single large one. These are drawn not just from London itself but from towns throughout the south and even further afield. While at home they tend to keep themselves to themselves, on their travels they join together under the collective blue banner to form a massive hard-core following.

The favoured tactic among the Chelsea hooligans is an old and established one. With such large numbers following the club, it makes it easy for them to just turn up and simply flood the area around the opposition ground. However, whereas the non-violent Chelsea supporters will arrive about one-ish, the mobs will turn up seriously early, sometimes even the night before, and will take up positions in the pubs and cafes normally used by their opposite numbers. Mobs will be stationed along the main routes to the ground to harass both the opposing fans and the police, put everyone on their guard and, more importantly, instil a certain degree of fear into their enemy. It is always down to the home lads to find the opposition and take the lead; and by using such tactics, Chelsea will have the upper hand and stop the rival mobs from firming up. It's simple, but it works. From within those large numbers who travel with the Blues, one group emerged to become one of the most feared football firms in Europe, the Chelsea Headhunters.

The Headhunters came to the notice of most supporters in the early eighties when groups of fans began to organise themselves into travelling mobs. Unlike many of the more infamous firms of that time, the Headhunters quickly became renowned for being more interested in dishing out actual violence than gaining a 'victory' over opposing fans. With a hard-core numbering in the region of 30 to 50, the firm soon became notorious. They set up a building society account to fund their travel and pay their fines, and their activities became so well-organised that they soon came under the watchful gaze of the boys in blue.

The police kept a close eye on the Headhunters and firmly believed that the group were actually funding their football activities through crime. Indeed, during the early eighties they had them down for numerous offences ranging from burglary to rape. The fact that the group usually travelled club-class when they flew, wore smart suits and listed their occupations as 'company director' – even though they apparently did not work at all – made them all the more interesting, not to mention mysterious. This profile, and their continuing role in the spread of football-related violence, made them a prime target during 'Own Goal', the fatally flawed anti-hooligan undercover operation.

When the police finally made their move against the Head-hunters, they arrested many of the alleged ringleaders and effectively broke the back of the group. However, when these individuals were released on appeal in November 1989, things quickly reverted to normal. By the time Italia 90 came around, the mob had regrouped with a hard-core of around 20, all very serious and extremely violent individuals. With approximately another 60 on the fringes, this mob was more than capable of causing serious problems, often with a distinctive, political motivation. As we have already mentioned, Chelsea have long had a right-wing following, something that dates back to the skinhead era of the late sixties. This made the club a prime target for the recruiters of both the National Front and the British National Party and, as we have seen, these groups enjoyed varying degrees of success at Stamford Bridge over the years. This right-wing influence, and the patriotic doctrine that accompanied it, meant that Chelsea supporters became very active with the England side in the eighties. They were roundly condemned when members of the Headhunters allegedly orchestrated mass abuse of the black players forcing their way into the national side at the time. Following their participation in numerous incidents at home and abroad, with both club and country, the Headhunters had become firmly established as one of the top four or five hooligan groups in the country, and their activities during Italia 90 saw them return as probably *the* top firm in England. However, while the group were already regarded by all as one of the more extreme right-wing firms, everything was to take on a new dimension in 1992 when a new organisation called 'Combat 18' was formed.

For many football fans, Combat 18 *are* the Chelsea Head-hunters. Although this may not be strictly true – clubs throughout the country have pockets of support that align themselves to Combat 18 – it would be fair to say that many of C18's top boys watch their football at Stamford Bridge and have been involved with the Headhunters in the past.

In the early nineties, the political leanings of the Headhunters, linked as they were with C18, led them to forge a number of links with hooligan firms in Scotland, Rangers being the prime example due to their shared loyalist connections. This led to members of the group being invited to travel to Scotland to take part in trouble, and we have been told of at least one occasion at an 'Old Firm' game at Parkhead when the main Celtic firm, hearing rumours of a combined Rangers–Headhunters mob, bottled out completely. The group also forged links with Hearts, another Scottish firm with a right-wing element, and in 1993 the police announced that they had tracked 30 known Headhunters to Belgium, where they had joined up with Hearts' CSF (Casual Soccer Firm) to fight rival supporters. At this point, the police made it known that they believed that the Headhunters were actually hiring themselves out to other football firms in need of numbers and, more importantly, fighters.

By now, even other Chelsea supporters were becoming wary of the group. In 1994, the Headhunters were linked with at least two particularly violent attacks on members of the Chelsea

Independent Supporters Association (CISA), who refused to accept right-wing literature for their fanzine. The first of these took place at a pub in Fulham when the group used pool balls at close range, resulting in various injuries including a broken jaw, broken nose and fractured skull. The second, and even more violent attack took place in Prague after a Cup-Winners' Cup tie when the Headhunters attacked another Chelsea supporters' club coach, seriously injuring one particular member of the CISA. It was acts such as this that began attracting the attention of the British news media, but within a matter of months, a single incident was to bring the Headhunters and C18 to the attention of the entire footballing world – Dublin.

Looking back, it is clear that the two groups were *the* instigators of the trouble at the Ireland–England fixture. While it must be stated that the actual violence also involved many fans who held no strong political beliefs, the consequence for C18 was that it gained huge amounts of the one thing it craved: publicity. The sudden interest in right-wing political groups ensured that the media were all over C18, and by association the Headhunters. This soon filtered through to football in general, because on the horizon was a golden opportunity for these groups to make another political statement, Euro 96.

The right-wing elements were the unknown quantity during the build-up to the summer of 1996. The entire population had seen at first hand the possible threat that they held, and the prospect of extreme European political groups coming to England to take them on was a very real one.

In the event, the Headhunters kept a fairly low profile compared to many other groups although they were out and about, along with pockets of C18 from other clubs, certainly at the Globe in Baker Street which soon became *the* meeting place for England fans to seen in. Since the Euro 96 tournament came to an end, the group have kept fairly quiet and seem to have settled back into the routine (as if there is such a thing) mob activities at games. The fact remains that the Chelsea Headhunters are a scary group of individuals, possibly the most dangerous in English football, and it is certain that they will make the headlines again. Take care.

PART THREE
West Ham United

Chapter 5
The Footballing Academy

It used to be an unwritten rule in the closed community of the East End of London that there were two things no outsider should be allowed to do: sell on the markets and drink in the pubs. Over the years, of course, largely as a result of the shifting population, both of these 'traditions' have been eroded, but there is another rule that remains as strictly enforced as ever: no one without roots in the East End should support West Ham. There is no doubt that Hammers fans are among the most fiercely loyal in the country and this loyalty runs deep. Very deep.

West Ham United were an integral part of East End culture in the early part of this century. In an area that had more than its fair share of poverty, the club quickly became entrenched in the local community from which, incidentally, it drew almost all of its players. Following the Second World War, the carpet-bombing of the East End had left not only most of the docks but also many of the homes and streets severely, if not irreparably, damaged. As a result, whole communities were forced to move eastward, towards Grays, Romford and Tilbury, but their unique community spirit and loyalty to the old East End remained. For many, the best way those links could be kept alive was via West Ham United Football Club. In the fifties and early sixties, the redevelopment of London, and the East End in particular, saw yet more families leave the city and move out to the New Towns east of London, such as Basildon. As these communities left, the club became even more of a focus for them, and their loyal support and allegiance have been passed down through the generations to the point where, unlike most of the other London clubs, West Ham rivals Liverpool and Newcastle insomuch as if your dad supports the Irons, so do you and so will your sons. That's the way West Ham is, and long may it remain so.

As most people are aware, the East End has always been a bit of a rough area. Crime has always been a fact of life there, and where you get any amount of crime, violence will never be far away. This inevitably found its way to Upton Park and the club soon became famous for having a volatile and sometimes hostile following. The supporters had been involved in numerous incidents of violence in the early part of the century, but it was not until the sixties that it began to get really serious.

It was a decade which saw Upton Park gain a reputation as a rough ground to visit. The rise in serious incidents throughout football in England was dramatic and West Ham were implicated in more than one of these.

The first incident of note involved a club that, to the Hammers fans, has become one of the fiercest rivals over the years, Manchester United. In May 1967, United came to East London needing to beat West Ham to claim the Championship. With them they brought thousands upon thousands of supporters, in what was basically an invasion of East London. This was met with a great deal of anger and resistance by both the West Ham fans and the locals generally, and fighting soon broke out in a number of pubs. Following the game, which Man United won 6–1, their fans spilled out onto the streets to begin their celebrations. However, in the event they ended up trashing almost everything in sight, which infuriated the locals even more. Fighting broke out again and continued for many hours. Subsequently, word went out that Manchester United had 'taken' East London and it was this that finally shook the Hammers fans into action.

At the start of the 1967–68 season, August Bank Holiday in fact, West Ham travelled to Tottenham and their supporters went on the rampage. Prior to the game, they had been causing all sorts of trouble around North London, with numerous minor disturbances causing problems for the police. However, following the game, which West Ham lost 5–1, the Hammers fans went crazy. Mobs of them stormed down the streets outside the ground, smashing windows and damaging property. The police soon brought in reinforcements, including dogs and a riot van, and arrested seventeen people before getting the supporters onto a number of trains back to East London. But the West Ham fans had not finished their big day out and fighting continued on the trains, resulting in at least one being taken out of service due to the vandalism. West Ham fans caused trouble at almost every away fixture that year, as they built for themselves a fearsome reputation.

As football violence spread throughout the country, the West Ham followers were considered by the authorities to be among the very worst in the land. At the 1975 FA Cup final against Fulham, some of them invaded the hallowed turf and taunted Fulham fans at the opposing end. This then spilled over into fighting outside the ground and on the underground, bringing heaps of condemnation down on the club from all sides. The fact that this had happened at Wembley seemed too much for everyone to bear.

Police forces throughout England were being placed on high alert every time West Ham came to town. Their fans' unpredictability left local communities in fear, while a return visit to the East End was viewed as something undertaken only by the very brave or the brain-dead.

Millwall were always the obvious 'local' rivals for West Ham, not just in terms of geography but also because they, like the Hammers, are an integral part of East London, having their roots in the docks. This has meant that the two sets of supporters, traditionally among the most violent in England anyway, have been involved in some terrible incidents over the years. The events of December 1976 are especially remembered for the first fatality involving the two sets of fans. Following trouble before and during the game, three Millwall fans chased two West Ham supporters onto a train at New Cross station and a fight started.

The West Ham fans managed to force two of the Millwall supporters off the train and then set about the third as revenge. As he fell to the floor, one of the West Ham fans opened the door on the far side of the train and the other pushed him out into the path of an oncoming express. He was killed instantly. This, as you can imagine, sent shock-waves through the game. It had taken hooliganism to a previously unimagined level. The Police Federation chairman, already concerned at the rising level of violence in and around stadia, called for football to be suspended for a year to stop hooliganism once and for all. However, despite this appeal and the fact that those concerned were prosecuted, things continued largely unchecked.

West Ham supporters continued to wreak havoc wherever they went, building on an already unenviable reputation week by week. In November 1978 they went on the rampage again, this time in Leicester.

LEICESTER

Leicester '78, that was the first time I ended up in the cells so I remember it well! We'd gone up there well tooled-up. They had a nice little mob of lads themselves and we needed the added help, getting tooled-up was nothing unusual.

There was loads of trouble on the train with the Transport Police. They were all over us at that time, and when we got to Leicester they took a few lads way for smashing things up during the journey. We arrived about mid-morning and hung around the station for more lads to arrive, but Leicester were there already, waiting for us, and it kicked off straight away. The police soon sorted it out and held us in the station while they saw off the home lads. Then they let us go.

We were in this pub, I'll never forget it, the Saracen's Head, when all hell broke loose and there were bottles and glasses flying everywhere. The Leicester lads had tracked us down and had come looking for it. West Ham run from no one, that was the motto, and even though there were more of them, we stood firm and fought like fuck. That pub was a mess inside and out, but the thing I remember was this lad, one of theirs, that had been slashed down the side. That was the most blood I'd ever seen. The police came but didn't arrest or search anyone, even after something like that.

We were forced down to the ground by the coppers, but about 20 of us got away from the escort and went looking for something to eat. Well, we turned this corner and saw a massive off outside this cafe. Loads of Leicester lads were outside, so it was obvious it was more of our lot inside. The window was put through and all the West Ham lads were jumping out through the empty pane as the home lads threw bottles and stuff at them. There were a couple of our lot that got well turned-over there.

At the ground, we met up with all the other lads and it was obvious that West Ham had been everywhere in the town and turned the place over. Apart from our stuff, there had been loads of offs, including one in the shopping centre which was apparently a corker. Anyway, we were queuing to get in when we noticed that the police were searching everyone, rare in those days. All you could hear was the sound of weapons being dropped on the floor, knives, coshes, the lot. It was quite funny, really. You could have opened a market stall with that lot.

Anyway, inside the ground was mad. Our lads were brilliant, loads of noise and really up for it. A few of their lads were near us giving it the big 'un, and in the end it went off again and I was nicked. This copper grabbed me, hauled me out and dragged me round the pitch. I really thought he was only going to throw me out, but he had my arm so far up my back it nearly came off and I was still struggling. Anyway, as we get near the home end, they start giving it loads and this lad gobbed on me – and I hate that more than anything. I'm struggling enough to get near to their lot, so I lashed out and kicked some lad right on the side of the head. They went mental and these other coppers came in, grabbed my legs and carried me out, one on each corner. Funny as fuck when you look back on it. I suppose it's got to happen to you at least once.

I ended up in the cells for the night with this Leicester tosser who spent the night bleating about Cockneys and West Ham fans in general, he drove me nuts. There were loads of Hammers in the other cells and they told us that the local magistrates were having a special sitting on the Monday morning to deal with us all. There was no way I was playing up any more, which was a good thing really because in the end they kicked me out the next morning without charge.

For most East Enders, the seaside means only one place, Southend-on-Sea. So it surely comes as no surprise to find that this club in particular has seen West Ham fans at their most fearsome. While competitive fixtures between the two clubs are rare, due to the fact that they are usually in different divisions, the close proximity of the place to East London makes it an almost compulsory pre-season friendly for West Ham. It also means a pre-season warm-up for the fans, and in early August 1979 they descended on the town and caused mayhem. Trouble initially erupted along the seafront, but once the game started it quickly resurfaced in the ground, during which time the police ejected numerous West Ham fans, nine of whom were caught on the roof of the main stand, presumably attempting to get at the Southend supporters.

Following the game, the trouble spread to the streets and the pubs, but the most vicious incident took place at the Palace Hotel where the manager had refused to allow West Ham fans into the bar. Unfortunately, a small number had managed to sneak in and were soon boasting about how they had given one Southend supporter a kicking earlier in the day. When the manager realised they were there, and sensed the potential trouble they could cause, he went to eject them. This led to a heated argument in the middle of which one of the West Ham fans broke a billiard-cue across the manager's head while the rest used snooker balls and glasses in a frenzied attack on him. When the police arrived, the manager had suffered severe cuts and bruises but the Hammers fans were merely told to leave and none was arrested.

That same season, the two of us were to encounter the West Ham boys for the first time at Vicarage Road and it was not a pleasant experience. They quite simply came to Watford to put on a massive show of force and certainly succeeded. The police at the time estimated that West Ham brought in the region of 7,000 fans with them, and although trouble before the match was limited, it quickly became apparent that they had infiltrated every section of the ground and the home end in particular. Although the police were all over the place, trouble started when the West Ham fans in the home end began chanting for their team before the kick-off. I have never seen so many away fans in any home section as West Ham had up the Vicarage Road end that day; they must have numbered in the region of 1,000. Their early showing allowed the police time to move many of them out before the main influx of Watford fans came into their normal enclosure. During the game, numerous fights erupted, with Watford fans certainly holding their own as they got to what West Ham lads were left, though admittedly there were only a few. As the match and the fighting wore on, the West Ham fans in the away enclosure, wanting a piece of the action, invaded the pitch and threw missiles at the home fans.

Following the game, a group of around 200 West Ham escaped the police escort back to the station and set out on what the local papers called 'an orgy of destruction'. Windows were smashed and cars damaged by this mob, who also fought with groups of Watford fans. In truth, everyone was astonished at their afternoon's work.

A 1–0 win over Arsenal in the 1980 FA Cup final saw West Ham qualify for European competition. Their hooligans now had a new arena in which to display their own particular style of support. It was an opportunity they were never going to let pass them by.

September 1980 was to be a rough month for West Ham and their supporters. On the first Saturday of the month they travelled to Stamford Bridge, where the favoured Hammers tactic of infiltration resulted in numerous outbreaks of fighting on the home terraces. Forty-two were arrested and two policemen were taken to hospital, but while this was bad enough, of greater concern to the club was the forthcoming trip to Spain for a European Cup-Winners' Cup tie against Castilla. The FA and UEFA had made it clear that any trouble involving English supporters abroad would be treated with the utmost seriousness, in the light of the riot involving England fans in Turin earlier that summer. The club, terrified at the thought of the possible repercussions, set out to ensure that things would go smoothly. They sold tickets only to registered supporters who were photographed and had their passport numbers noted, while Billy Bonds, the Hammers captain, wrote to every travelling fan, pleading for them to behave. However, hundreds of supporters made their own way from the East End and, as usual, were able to buy tickets in Spain, causing untold problems for the local police.

The inevitable trouble initially started in a number of bars where some West Ham fans became drunk and abusive. This continued right up to the actual match, where fans fought with police while those in the upper tier of the Bernabeu Stadium spat and urinated on the Spanish supporters below. Outside the ground, an eighteen-year-old West Ham fan was, according to the Hammers supporters, deliberately run down by a Spanish coach driver, with the result that it all kicked off again. UEFA were furious and handed the club a hefty fine, as well as ordering them to play the return leg behind closed doors, even though they acknowledged that the club had done everything it could to prevent trouble.

While the European excursion was relatively short-lived, winning the Second Division Championship that same season saw the club return to the top flight. That meant fresh opponents for the West Ham supporters, and as every firm in the country tried to enhance their own reputations, the Irons were seen as a top target. Unfortunately for some, not every plan worked out quite as it was meant to. C. H. tells all.

* * *

EVERTON

In 1981 we were drawn to play West Ham in the FA Cup here at Goodison Park. West Ham were *the* mob then, and to a fourteen-year-old boy this added the chance of seeing a big row to the day, something that wasn't going to be missed.

I had gone along with my mates as usual, all of us still at school but thinking we were the bees' knees and well hard. The atmosphere at the game was fantastic, really tense. The local bizzies never had a clue in those days, as no respecting scally would wear a scarf. The Everton lads used the same tactic every week and would go into the Park End stand with the away fans unnoticed and kick it off. That tactic was particularly successful against Arsenal in the Cup, but our lads came unstuck when Man United proved to be a bit harder than the Londoners and gave the Blues a good kicking. The Man U mob were the top team to come to Everton in those days, always causing loads of trouble.

West Ham had a big mob themselves that day, but as expected our lads steamed into them. Watching football violence is fantastic, it really gets you going seeing lads chase each other all over the place, trying to beat the fuck out of each other. The two mobs put up a really good show – and once the bizzies decided to turn up, they got in on it as well, whacking people and dragging them out. They don't seem to do that so much now in the ground; I suppose it's because they could get caught on video as well as anyone, although I'd be surprised if that bit of film would make it to the magistrates' court. At that time I had never been involved because I was too young. We did keep a lookout for away fans in the park for the lads in the pub, but that was about it. The whole crowd was watching and cheering the boys on. Everyone hated the Londoners then. Most people still do up here, and think of them as flash, thick wankers.

The bizzies brought the dogs in and that soon sorted things out and kept it all quiet until after the match. Word was going around that there was to be a massive off after the game. The lads were saying that the West Ham boys were carrying knives and had tried to slice a few people up. This put the shits up me – well, I was only fourteen at the time – but we decided to hang around the edges and see if we could taste our first real bit of action.

The police kept the Londoners in for ages. There were loads of lads hanging around and the bizzies were doing their best to break our mob up before letting them out. We went around to Priory Road with our pockets full of stones to throw at the coaches (our other favourite pastime in those days) but the bizzies had blocked them off as well and we couldn't really get near it. The mob grew so big that the bizzies had to charge us with the horses to get us away. They loved the chance to give us a few smacks back then, and they did it with great gusto, the bastards. About half the lads got chased up Stanley Road and we ran down the hill onto County Road. The meat-trucks were piling down after us as well, and they were trying to pull lads in the back and take them down the nick. It was scary but fucking great fun at the time. This was it, we were in with the lads, so we thought, having it away with the bizzies.

When we got to the bottom, everyone went along County Road so that we could meet up with the others at the foot of Everton Valley. As we approached the Valley, we could hear all the other lads in the distance.

We reached the corner and could see them coming down the hill, about 200 lads followed by the bizzies. Then they started to run at us. At first I thought they were running from the bizzies, but then they started to throw bottles and bricks at us and were screaming their heads off. I couldn't believe it, these were other Blues. I shit myself, I had never been so scared in all my life. All you could do was try and dodge the missiles by covering your head, and try to keep out of the way of the cars in the road at the same time. Windscreens were put through and a lad next to me got hit by a car as he tried to get out of the way. As the other lads got on top of us, he got booted in the head as he lay on the floor. He took a right beating from these twats, his own lot! Blokes were jumping out of their cars and fighting back as well, it was mental. The bizzies came flying in again and it was only then, as some of our lot were screaming, 'Everton, we're fucking Everton,' that they finally realised what was going on. Loads of lads had been hit and the odd bit kept going off as lads argued among themselves about what had happened and drivers had a go about their motors.

Again the bizzies started to nick people. I heard one lad shouting to the bizzy taking him away, 'You can't nick me for fighting with other Everton fans. You can't,' as if it were against the law. Soft twat. There were knives and all sorts of stuff left lying around.

I was so relieved it was over and wanted to get out of there more than anything else in the world. Then some coaches started to come towards Scotland Road and the Tunnel. To cap off a marvellous day, these twats began to get ready to brick what were obviously Everton fans going back to Birkenhead and the Wirral. A couple of stones were thrown but the lads who did it got a right mouthing. I've no idea what happened to the West Ham lads and they must have wondered where the hell we had gone, because they must have been looking for it somewhere as well.

Despite such a disastrous introduction to it all, I've become more and more involved in the violence. I can honestly say, that day was the most scary experience I've had at football. I've been twatted at Birmingham, chased all over Leeds, truncheoned at Maine Road and whacked at Highbury, but getting bricked by our own lads was something else.

The following year was to see another tragic landmark in the black history of the club's supporters, another death. On 1 May 1982, West Ham travelled to Highbury for a game against their rivals from North London. As was usual, trouble began early on in the day and there were a number of serious incidents on the tube as Arsenal fans attempted to gain control of their 'manor'. During the game, it soon became apparent that West Ham had got into every part of the ground. Fighting broke out on both the North Bank and the Clock End. West Ham fans let off smoke bombs causing mayhem, which eventually forced the game to be held up for ten minutes while calm was restored and supporters were cleared from the pitch. Following the match, trouble flared up again and it was during one such incident that a supporter was stabbed to death.

On their travels, the West Ham fans continued to play up. During a trip to Birmingham, trouble started at New Street station when the Birmingham fans were ambushed by Hammers supporters arriving early. It continued right up to the game and started again once play was underway. Following the match, the West Midlands Police, not known for their tolerance of football fans at the best of times, all but dragged the West Ham fans back to the station, but this time it was the Londoners who were ambushed and during the trouble that followed yet another supporter was stabbed. Later that year, Birmingham supporters mounted a huge revenge mission and travelled to London with a massive mob. However, word had got to the Hammers fans, who ambushed the Blues supporters at Euston and then harried them all the way to Upton Park, where fighting erupted first outside the ground and then while the game was underway. Such was the level of violence at this game that play was held up for almost 20 minutes while the police restored order. During the journey back to Euston, the supporters again attacked each other and it took a concerted effort from the British Transport Police to get the Birmingham fans onto the train and out of London. Yet another feud had been established.

That same season, the West Ham supporters descended on Brighton for a match that was to see trouble on a scale that surprised even many of those who travelled. As is usual when the club play at the seaside, the fans began travelling on the Friday and by early evening, groups totalling approximately 400 were roaming the town looking for somewhere to drink. This resulted in a number of incidents, including one where a local youth was slashed from ear to ear before being stabbed in the back and the chest. Another man was battered about the head with a crowbar. Later that evening, a seafront cafe was looted and a boat went up in flames. On the Saturday, fighting began quite early in the day and 55 supporters were arrested before the game, charged with offences ranging from threatening behaviour, assault and obstruction to possession of offensive weapons. Immediately before the match another twelve were arrested, including a woman who had a dart in her pocket. Fighting broke out in the home end before a ball was kicked, as the West Ham fans made their presence felt. Early on in the game, a crush-barrier collapsed and numerous scuffles broke out, but these were quickly contained by the police, who arrested a further 41 supporters during the game. Following the match, the police amazingly managed to get the West Ham fans back to the station without further incident.

By now the Inter City Firm (ICF) was a household name thanks to their exploits, and the following season (1983–84), the West Ham hooligans, now under intense scrutiny from the police and the media, set out on what was to be probably their worst year. There were, by this time, numerous feuds festering within the Football League, and West Ham were involved in almost all of them. Hardly a week went by without their supporters being involved in something, but the three worst incidents that season all involved old foes. Their first targets were to be Tottenham.

West Ham and Spurs had been involved in numerous confrontations over the years, but the East End club usually had the upper hand. On most Saturdays, West Ham supporters would travel to North London to take on either Arsenal or Spurs, at Euston or on the tube, to make sure that their local rivals knew they hadn't been forgotten. It was during a return trip from Everton that a leaflet was found by a West Ham fan which stated that the Tottenham fans were going to mob-up at the Corner Pin pub on Tottenham High Road the following Saturday, which just happened to be the West Ham game. The leaflet went on to say that the reputation of the Spurs fans depended on their performance against West Ham, and that they would have to get a result because 'West Ham think we're soft'. The information spread rapidly through the West Ham ranks and they spent the week making plans. It had already been decided to infiltrate and take 'The Shelf' at White Hart Lane, but this leaflet gave them fresh ideas.

On Saturday 3 September 1983, the Spurs fans gathered outside the Corner Pin and Bell and Hare pubs in Tottenham High Road, totally unaware that the West Ham fans knew they would be mobbing-up. The police, unaware of anything, had only a token presence in the area, but they were becoming concerned at the increasing numbers of West Ham fans moving into North London. (The West Ham lads always liked to attack early, as this meant the opposition hadn't usually got their full mob out.) At about eleven o'clock, the 30 or so Spurs fans outside the pubs suddenly came under attack as a massive West Ham mob hit them from both sides. After about five minutes of intensive and very violent fighting, the Spurs fans managed to regroup and staged a counter-attack. After an hour of running battles, with more and more hooligans joining the fray, mounted police and three bus-loads of officers managed to drive the fans apart. They pinned the Hammers fans against a wall, where they were kept until the gates were opened at one o'clock.

The West Ham fans had certainly had a good result. They had come to Spurs in numbers and gone for it. The Spurs fans were incensed, but worse was to come. At about 2.20 p.m. inside the ground, a glass was thrown on The Shelf, which was the signal for the West Ham mobs to show themselves. It was immediately clear that the ICF had infiltrated the home stand and, as soon as they made their presence known, the non-violent home fans were sent into a blind panic. The police were quickly on the scene and dragged a number out, but after another five minutes it went off again and this was the pattern for the rest of the match. The West Ham fans were jubilant. Chants of 'West Ham run from no one' and 'ICF, ICF' rang out from the Spurs terraces throughout the game, while the Spurs hooligans, penned back by the police, were enraged.

Following the game, the police drove the two sets of fans apart but the rival mobs made their way to the tube and fighting erupted at both Euston and Victoria. The Hammers fans now believed, with some justification, that they really were the top boys. The fact that they stood firm and never ran from opposing groups was a proven fact, as was their unpredictability. No one knew what they would get up to next, and many fans, faced with a visit to Upton Park, never found out. They simply didn't go.

Millwall were the next targets for the West Ham firm and were hit when they were least expecting it, on their way to another game. The violence flared when Millwall fans, waiting for a train taking them to their Third Division match against Sheffield United, were ambushed by West Ham at London Bridge station. A petrol-bomb was thrown down onto the platform by a West Ham fan, but thankfully, no one was injured. However, the subsequent violence included fans fighting with bottles, bricks and even the old East End favourite, meat-cleavers. A ticket collector was injured by flying glass and an innocent passenger hit on the forehead by a flying bottle. The police, like the Millwall fans, were totally unprepared for this attack and took an age to arrive, but even when they did, it took a considerable time for them to separate the groups, who had caused severe damage to the station. Despite the fact that seven fans were arrested, West Ham had again shown that they were ready and able to take on anyone, anywhere, and at any time.

In February 1984, the Hammers were handed the chance to sort out Birmingham City and their fledgling 'Zulu Army'. The club that had given the West Ham fans such trouble only two seasons before were drawn against them in the FA Cup and came down to Upton Park, where they were faced with a massive police operation designed to keep the two sets of fans apart. While to a certain degree the police were successful, fans still fought on the tube and a number of potentially fatal incidents, including one at Euston where a Birmingham fan was stabbed, were only contained by a concerted operation staged by the British Transport Police. Inside the ground, other problems quickly surfaced. On the pitch, West Ham found themselves behind and the fans, decidedly unhappy, staged a mass pitch-invasion in an attempt to get the game abandoned. The first encroachment was soon dealt with, but then a second attempt was made soon afterwards. However, the referee made it clear that whatever happened, the game would be finished. In the event, over 100 people were injured during the fighting at this game, which West Ham lost 3–0. But it was the pitch invasions that had finally pushed the FA too far.

Lancaster Gate was beside itself with rage. The season had already been one of the worst to date, with serious crowd violence at Ayresome Park and Brighton, Spurs fans rioting in Rotterdam and England fans on the rampage in Luxembourg (not to mention the Hammers fans' activities at almost every ground they visited). The club was threatened with a two-year ban from the FA Cup if its fans did not start behaving, but unbelievably, the club appealed. Even more unbelievably, they won and the threat was lifted. By now, even UEFA were concerned and the FA were told in no uncertain terms that English clubs would be banned from European competition if they did not sort things out, and sort them out quickly.

While all of this was going on, two things were taking place that would prove to be of great significance for both the West Ham fans and, more specifically, the Inter City Firm. The first was that the group were now the target of a major undercover police operation; the second was that they were the subject of what was to become a legend among football mobs everywhere, the Thames Television documentary, *Hooligan*. The concept of both of these ideas was actually very similar: follow the West Ham firm around and see what they got up to. But as it happened, one was a good deal more successful than the other. In the case of the police operation, the evidence submitted to the Department of Public Prosecutions proved to be so fatally flawed that they eventually decided (in 1988) to drop all charges against seventeen of the ICF's so-called top boys, a decision no doubt influenced by the farce that was Operation 'Own Goal', involving Chelsea fans.

The documentary was a different matter altogether and when it was shown, in August 1985, it succeeded in elevating the West

Ham supporters, and in particular the ICF, to a whole new level of infamy. The fighting groups, previously unknown to those outside football (not to mention many of those within it), were now put on show. It seemed that the rumours and the fears were all true, and the West Ham hooligans revelled in it. The media were now obsessed with football supporters, not just at Upton Park but at most of the big clubs, and were 'exposing' hooligan groups at almost every club in England. The publicity suddenly given to the ICF had seen copycat groups spring up overnight, and that, along with the infamous Millwall riot at L*t*n only five months earlier, prompted the government to go on the offensive against the hooligans.

The year 1985 was a terrible one for football. L*t*n, Bradford, Heysel, the death of a Birmingham fan at St Andrews, the banning of English clubs from Europe, the list went on and on. The government, and in particular Mrs Thatcher, made it clear that football had to clean up its act or she would do it for them. The result of this was that clubs finally began looking towards prevention rather than reaction. Identity-card schemes and the banning of away fans were among the ideas put forward (and subsequently dumped), but it was to be the increasing use of closed-circuit television (CCTV) that was to be the key weapon inside grounds. Ironically, West Ham had been one of the early pioneers of CCTV. In the early eighties, a very basic system had been installed at Upton Park and had been instrumental in the ejection of numerous individuals.

For the West Ham fans intent on violence, things were becoming difficult. The police, still believing that the use of more undercover operations was a good idea, were all over the club like a rash, which made not only confrontation but even travel difficult for the mobs. The fans, renowned for being one step ahead, soon found ways to fool the Old Bill, including the use of something that was to become a favourite toy, the mobile phone. The hooliganism problem was far from over and 1986 was to see yet another incident involving West Ham fans that quickly proved the point.

In May of that year, FIFA announced that it was relaxing the ban on English clubs playing pre-season friendlies in Europe. This tentative move was designed primarily to test out the anti-hooligan measures which had been implemented by the British government, but of course it also meant more money for the clubs. A number duly planned a series of matches abroad and just before the start of the following season, West Ham and Manchester United headed off to Europe for some warm-up matches. What they did not do was consider the travel arrangements of the supporters, who were left to organise things themselves. In August 1986, a ferry sailed from Harwich to the Hook of Holland, a journey that normally takes about eight and a half hours. On board were approximately 130 football fans, and although the ferry company concerned had an unwritten rule not to carry football supporters, they were sure that there would be no trouble because they believed that the fans were all from the same club.

Unfortunately, out of the 130 fans, the 30 were West Ham and the other 100 Manchester United, and following a number of arguments in the bars, fighting soon erupted. With no police of any kind on board, the Dutch crew struggled to regain control of the situation and things steadily deteriorated until the captain decided that he would have to turn back to Harwich and get the police on board. With the boat already two and a half hours into its journey, the crew still faced another two and a half hours of violence on the way back, and the supporters were soon at it with fire hoses, bottles and knives. When the boat finally docked, the police arrested 14 supporters while another four were taken to hospital with stab wounds and a further 20 or 30 had injuries caused by broken glass and punches. Neither the FA nor UEFA were amused, with UEFA stating that English clubs were indeed the worst in Europe and they could see no way for them to be readmitted for at least another year.

The West Ham fans, now firmly in the public eye and happy in the knowledge that 30 of their own had 'got a result' when outnumbered over three-to-one, set out on the new season with some verve. For them it would be yet another year of violence, including a spectacular attack on Chelsea fans in a market-place, where they used bottles and crates. Chelsea were hit again on the tube with iron bars and knives, and Sheffield Wednesday fans were attacked at Sheffield station using ball-bearings, knives and ammonia. The club's supporters were even involved in a disturbance at the Wembley Arena following a boxing match involving Mark Kaylor from West Ham and Herol 'Bomber' Graham.

The police, after years of shadowing the club's fans, were now intent on snuffing out the hooligan following and arrested eleven alleged ringleaders in early 1987. They were charged with various offences dating back to 1980. As we have already seen, these charges were eventually dropped, but the fans were somewhat shaken by all of this and things began to calm down a little. However, in October 1989 the supporters were involved in an incident that ranks as one of the more bizarre episodes in hooligan history. The following account was supplied by John W., a West Ham fan living in Birmingham.

MOTORWAY MADNESS

We hadn't played Birmingham for a few years, what with them being in the Second Division, and then we drew them in a Cup tie. The lads were all delirious, I mean over the years there had been some right offs with them. The word went out that a lot of lads would be coming up by train but loads more would come up by coach to avoid the police, who at that time were real bastards. Anyway, although a few things went off outside the ground, there was nothing like the trouble we had had before when the Hammers played there – but the reason for that was that loads of our coaches had been held up on the Aston Expressway and it had all gone off on the motorway. Apparently, it all started when a load of Blues fans began giving it the biggie when they overtook the West Ham coaches, but when they got caught in traffic, the West Ham lads steamed off and totalled their car. Then all these others joined in and that was it, running battles on the fucking motorway!

* * *

Just over a year later, pitched battles involving the club's followers made yet another unwelcome return to the back pages. On 12 November 1990, West Ham travelled to The Den, home of Millwall, and the sheer scale of the fighting at this game was extraordinary. At one point, the police estimated that there were 400 people fighting outside the ground, and one battle lasted 25 minutes before the police could separate the warring factions. Cars and houses were damaged with flying bricks and bottles, and in all 15 people were injured, including a policeman stabbed with a syringe. The police, who were totally unprepared for the scale of this riot, announced the next day that this was 'just like the bad old days'. Indeed, reports at the time stated that, having driven the fans apart, they were then attacked by both sets of supporters simultaneously. By taking such a massive mob to Cold Blow Lane and fronting up their most hated rivals, the West Ham hooligans had gained another major victory.

From that point on, the club's hooligan following retreated into a regular pattern, with the matchday madness never far from the surface and always under that watchful eye of the boys in blue. But the increasing use of weapons became a specific worry and the West Ham firm were one of the first to use CS gas sprays, something that has since become a more regular occurrence at football. They have continued to enhance their reputation and have continued several long-standing feuds, not just those we have mentioned but with other clubs such as Middlesbrough, Liverpool and Newcastle. Indeed, back in the eighties, the Newcastle firm were involved in the firebombing of West Ham fans at St James' Park and they have also been very active when they visit Upton Park, putting up a big show on more than one occasion.

It is likely that at some time or another, most football fans will have had some experience of a West Ham mob. It isn't just the fact that West Ham are a mob who know the score, it is that they are so intent on getting a result. The East End of London is a hard place, and the football club provides an avenue in which to prove that point to the rest of the country.

Chapter 6

The Inter City Firm

Whenever the subject of organised football violence is discussed, one group inevitably gets a mention: the Inter City Firm, probably the first serious, organised hooligan mob and certainly the most infamous. This is no accident, as the group have been involved in numerous incidents of organised violence at almost every club in England over the years. Indeed, as their reputation preceded them, the mere threat of their arrival would sometimes see rival groups dissolve on the spot. The ICF have a long history of conflict, of which they are very proud for it has been hard won. Yet at the same time, surprisingly little is really known about them, and what is known is often dismissed as fiction or myth. Indeed, the phrase 'That's all bollocks' could well have been invented by the ICF – but if you look back over the years at their exploits, fact certainly outshines fiction.

Unlike certain other clubs (Chelsea being a good example), the supporters' groups tended to avoid splitting into separate factions on the terraces, despite the Hammers having a long and colourful history of trouble involving their fans. However, in the sixties, a group emerged from within that support who were keen to ensure that West Ham fans took an active role in the spread of terrace violence. This soon became a major problem for both the club and the police, because for the local hooligans, the defence of both their own small part of London and their burgeoning reputation became an essential part of the occasion.

As the police began to get some sort of grip on the fans' activities, the hard-core support forged itself into a gang, initially called the 'Mile End Mob' and then the 'Mile End Death Squad'. This group were bad enough, but as things progressed through the seventies and into the eighties, the increasingly high profile of the club's fans saw the emergence of the Inter City Firm, named after their preferred method of travel which in itself was a vital part of their armoury. By avoiding the usual coaches and specials, they distanced themselves from the 'average' supporter while remaining one step ahead of the police who fought to control them. Initially, the group were renowned for wearing a uniform of sorts, a cross between the 'skinhead' and 'suede' movements of the era: short hair and green fatigues. But as the casual movement began, the West Ham hooligans embraced it with open arms and were soon at the forefront of the fashion scene. As we have seen, the casual movement had other benefits for all the hooligan groups, because the expensive designer clothes made the wearing of colours a non-starter and the police in most cases had no idea what club the supporters were from, or indeed whether they were football fans at all! For the ICF, the specific attraction of the casual movement was that it made their favoured tactic of 'infiltration' even easier, and they used it to devastating effect almost every week.

The West Ham hooligans had always preferred to get into the opposing fans' end and kick it off, with the aim of totally humiliating them. This was fine on their travels, but at home things were different and here they favoured the use of intimidation, searching out visiting fans and making it clear that they had been seen and were in grave danger, merely for having had the nerve to come. Something guaranteed to relax the bowels! Eddy explains one visit to Upton Park.

GOING DOWN THE PARK

There are three grounds I really hate to visit. One is L*t*n, because it's shit; one is Bolton, because the coppers and the natives are nutty; and the other is Upton Park. Every time I had gone down there, I had been spotted on the walk down from the tube and my arse would go the size of a manhole cover as the little bastards pointed me out to the older lads. Well, one year I thought, fuck that, I'll bottle out and go on the coaches with the knobheads. This was all fine for me and my mate Steve until we got in the ground.

There were loads of West Ham in our bit and they were busy picking people off, so we went and hid well away from the rest. After about ten minutes, me and Steve are standing down the front when I felt a tap on the shoulder. I looked around and there must have been about fifteen faces all grinning at me from ear to ear, all West Ham. I'll never forget the words: 'We've seen you. You can't hide anymore.' They were so happy that they had found us. I only received one boot up the arse as I made my escape, but my pants had to go through the hot wash more than once.

The other thing almost unique to the group was that they were, and remain, fearless in their approach to football violence. They will not run or shy from anything and will do whatever it takes to get a result. This has meant that over the years, they have been involved in incidents that are regarded with disbelief even by those from other active groups.

The ICF has always maintained a hard-core of about 150, with up to 500 on the fringes and out for the big games. This has been supplemented by the use of the 'Under-Fives', lads in their mid-teens who do all the scouting and the winding-up but who are, nonetheless, ready to go for it should things happen. Indeed, on numerous occasions there have been serious offs on the tube involving the Under-Fives, and it has to be said that they have been a fair firm on their own over the seasons. However, in the early eighties, the ICF became known to the media for another feature of their membership, the 'City boys'.

The make-up of the ICF has always been uniquely East End. While traditionally this has meant that they have been working-class and poor, the City boom of the 1980s saw a number of East

End lads make good there, and they were often to be found inside Upton Park and with the ICF. This led to the group gaining a reputation as the 'Yuppie Firm', and the media made great play of the fact that here were lads who made massive fortunes, lived on the edge and used football to blow out the cobwebs (the inference being that their involvement in violence was therefore understandable and almost acceptable). It is certainly true that on their travels, the ICF weren't afraid to 'flash the cash'. They were also among the first to introduce mobile phones and 'calling cards'.

One of the early, high-profile uses of a calling card was the occasion in May 1982 when an Arsenal fan was stabbed to death. Pinned to his chest was a card with the legendary message, 'Congratulations, you have just met the Inter City Firm.' The media went crazy and, needless to say, their coverage simply ensured that within days, every named firm in the country were busy getting their own cards printed! An own goal, if ever there was one.

As the ICF became larger, more violent and better organised, so they also became more famous. The growing interest in football violence as an academic subject had seen the West Ham firm at the forefront of the 'investigations'. Various articles and books were published which talked about the group as if it were some weird social experiment, as the academics fought to outdo each other with more and more bizarre theories as to the root causes of the problem. This merely provided the ICF with more publicity, the thing they craved the most, and the sheer fear that the name inspired ensured that they almost always came out on top. While the police launched undercover operations against them, the ICF's profile was raised to new heights in 1985, as we have seen, by the now-famous television documentary, *Hooligan*. Overnight, the group became a household name and they revelled in their new-found status. (Plans were even put forward to copyright the initials ICF and market a brand of merchandise aimed at football fans around the country.) It seemed to many as if the group were almost untouchable, despite the government's insistence that the game must crack down on the hooligans and the organised groups once and for all. The ICF continued their activities almost un-checked, with riots, stabbings and the use of even more dangerous weaponry, such as CS gas, becoming almost routine.

Their image as a violent and fearless group made the ICF an obvious target for the right-wing political organisations, but unlike their Chelsea counterparts, they have always tended to resist such advances. There have been a number of reasons put forward for this, and most of those are conjecture, but it is clear that the group has always remained insular, preferring to remain apart and aloof from other firms. Also significant is the fact that many members of the ICF have been black, and the introduction of anything so obviously guaranteed to upset the status quo would be counter-productive. That is not to say that there aren't right-wing supporters within the group, because there un-doubtedly are, but probably not on the scale of other firms. Certainly they have never controlled the West Ham firm in the way that the right-wingers have at Chelsea.

However, the ICF were never shy in developing new ways to shock and indeed were known for being remarkably inventive in their approach to football violence. One example of this surfaced in the early nineties, when a well-known washing powder began offering free railway tickets in a marketing promotion, under the slogan: 'Surprise a friend this weekend.' Seeing this, the ICF obtained numerous tickets and eventually, a Millwall fan was stabbed in the chest through one of the offer packets with 'Nothing personal – the Inter City Firm' written on the back.

While all of this was going on, the police were still having no real impact on the activities of the group, but in 1991 they were nonetheless able to announce that they believed the ICF to be in decline. The police had always thought that the group were involved in criminal activities away from football and now went on the offensive, accusing the ringleaders of organising both illegal raves and unlicensed fights. However, the fact that the police made no real evidence available, nor any subsequent arrests, led many people to believe that they were, not to put too fine a point on it, 'pissing in the wind'. It is clear, though, that the imple-mentation of the Taylor Report, the increasing attentions of the police, the drug culture of the early nineties and the use of CCTV did have an impact on the group's activities inside grounds.

However, perhaps just as relevant was the fact that the early nineties saw the West Ham supporters become aware that the 'community' orientation of the club was being eroded. The infamous West Ham Bond Scheme drove a nail into the heart of the club, as the fans suddenly realised that the club they defended was no longer theirs; the money men had moved in and were trying to screw them. The club they loved did not love them back. The fans were becoming increasingly alienated from, and by, *their* club, and this left a sour taste in the mouth of many. The ICF, as a group, suffered more than most, and while the majority of supporters will see the removal of this element from the club as a good thing, it is clear that their demise is far from permanent. The Inter City Firm will always be there and remain fiercely allied to West Ham. They may not be as active as they were, but as with all the top firms throughout the country, when the big games come round, their appearance is almost guaranteed.

PART FOUR
Millwall

Chapter 7
No One Likes Us . . .

For those who do not like or who have no interest in football, the mere mention of the subject of football hooliganism provokes the inevitable question: 'Are you a Millwall fan, then?' Because as most people know, the supporters who have inhabited The Den over the years – both Old and New – have never been the best behaved.

For some, this is hardly surprising. The bulk of Millwall's support has always originated from the East End and the docks, traditionally the roughest and poorest parts of London. The combination of the two has seen the supporters develop a sort of 'patriotic' pride in both their local area and the club, and they have been more than happy to defend this should the situation arise. Any attack on Millwall Football Club has always been regarded as a personal attack on the fans, but in some ways the problem runs deeper than that.

Like West Ham, when the club was formed (in 1885 as Millwall Rovers) it soon became an integral part of the local community. Subsequent name changes (to Millwall Athletic and then plain Millwall) and a number of different grounds merely cemented this relationship, and by the time they moved to Cold Blow Lane in 1910, Millwall FC were as much a part of East London as the docks themselves. The club became a focus for those who lived in the area and, for many, their only escape from the poverty in which they lived. Thus, it assumed major importance for them and the success of the club became paramount. A more alarming aspect of this, however, was that those who visited Millwall were not always welcomed with open arms, primarily because they were seen to be 'knocking' the East End, and there were numerous incidents of violence before the second world war. The first major outbreak happened in 1920 when during a game against Newport, missiles rained down on the opposition keeper from among the home support. Unfortunately for him, he then steamed into the crowd to apprehend those who were throwing things at him and was kicked to the ground and beaten up for his trouble. The club were forced to close the ground for two weeks as punishment, something that was to happen with alarming regularity over the next 50 years. Indeed, the next such occasion was only fourteen years away. In 1934, the referee came under missile attack during a game against Bradford, which resulted in another two-week ban, while in 1938, the club were again fined for persistent crowd trouble involving their fans.

During the war, the docks and the local area received a horrific pounding from the German bombers and, as we have seen, many people were forced to move out of the area into the surrounding suburbs. Once hostilities were over, however, the rebuilding of London provided a great deal of employment, especially at the docks, enabling many of those who had left to return. The club had retained a sentimental link with the East End population and was still regarded by many as a vital part of the community.

It was not long before the crowd violence returned. In 1947, the ground received yet another closure notice and a £100 fine was imposed following trouble against Barnsley. As was normal in those days, in the absence of any real travelling support the focus of the crowd's anger was the officials, in this case one of the linesmen who was shot in the chest with an air-gun. The next ground-closure came just three years later, in 1950, and again it was the officials who came under attack. Following a game against Exeter City approximately 200 fans ambushed the referee outside the ground, resulting in another seven-day closure and a £1,000 fine.

By the early sixties, things were changing in Britain. The rebellious youth of the 'Teddy Boy' era were causing problems for society in general, and with transport becoming more readily available, travelling supporters were beginning to become a normal feature in football. From among that element, there quickly grew a minority intent on confrontation, and Millwall soon developed a reputation as a rough place for opposing fans to visit. Certainly the other London clubs, who had always taken fans down to Cold Blow Lane, were coming under increasing attack from the local supporters. The scale of this violence, and the nature of it, was never more evident than in 1965. Early in the season, a policeman was attacked by supporters on the pitch during the Wrexham fixture, and this rattled the police more than usual. They were now very concerned at the way things were going at the club and made sure that every game at The Den received their close attention. But the fans were now taking the trouble on the road as well, and the November London derby against Brentford saw football hooliganism touch a new low. There had already been fighting before the game, but during it, a hand-grenade came out of the Millwall enclosure and landed on the pitch. As it happened, the grenade was a dud, but no one was to know that at the time.

In April the following year, it was to be a player that bore the brunt of the fans' anger. Derek Dougan, having scored a last-minute equaliser for Wolves at The Den, turned to celebrate with a fan who had run onto the pitch. Unfortunately, the fan in question was from Millwall and promptly punched Dougan in the face before being apprehended by the police. In the year that England were to host, and eventually win, the World Cup, it was the last thing the FA needed; but there were no major repercussions for the club following this incident.

Millwall were now regarded by many as having the worst followers in the country, and for many visiting fans, the trip from New Cross station to The Den would provide one of the more scary interludes of their supporting lives. Violence involving Millwall fans continued almost unimpeded and with increasingly available and affordable travel, they were to indulge in hooliganism almost wherever they went. The wrecking of tube trains and 'specials' became almost routine. It was a rough time for the club, but also for the game in general. It is important to note that while Millwall were undoubtedly one of the worst offenders, there were numerous clubs who were finding themselves saddled with this problem, not least because of the huge amounts of news coverage being devoted to it.

By the mid-seventies, the reputation of the Millwall followers was all but carved in stone, but 1975 was to see another attack on an official – a linesman after the match – and also the stabbing of a Cardiff City supporter. Then in 1976, a Peterborough United player was punched in the face by a Millwall fan during a match. The supporters also staged a mass takeover of The Valley, running Charlton ragged and swamping the local area. While the exploits of the Millwall fans were common knowledge among the football-loving public, they were now thrust into the television spotlight in 1977 when they were featured on BBC Television's *Panorama*. The Millwall mobs were suddenly household names and assumed a level of infamy previously unimagined. Inevitably, they began to play up to this new-found image even more, if that were possible.

In 1978, the club received yet another ground-closure as a result of hooliganism. With the team already 3–0 down during an FA Cup quarter-final tie against Ipswich Town, the fans invaded the pitch in an effort to get the game abandoned. After an eighteen-minute delay, the game continued and Millwall lost 6–1, but the fans had not finished. During disturbances inside and outside the ground, 22 policemen were injured. The FA immediately closed the ground for two weeks, fined the club £1,500 and banned them from staging FA Cup ties for the next two seasons. The Ipswich manager, Bobby Robson, went on record in the press to say that he thought that flame-throwers should be turned on the Millwall fans, while the Ipswich players confessed that even before the match they had been very concerned for their safety because of the intimidating nature of Millwall's ground. In truth, this was far from a rare thing at The Den. Numerous players of the period refused to take corners when they played there, because they simply did not know what would happen, be it abuse or even something worse. For the visiting fans, things were even more dangerous. It was bad enough inside, but getting in and out was a nightmare.

In April 1980, the Easter holiday saw Millwall visit Southend. Many of the fans travelled down on Good Friday to make a weekend of it and it was not long before trouble erupted, not just involving Millwall and Southend fans but also groups of punks and skinheads who had all converged on the town. Thankfully, this trouble was fairly sparse but on the Monday of the game, the town was flooded with youths. The police, fearing the worst, split the groups and took as many football fans as they could find up to the ground. Meanwhile, they marched the other groups around until they got bored and left of their own accord. Trouble surrounding the football match was not far away, however. A small pocket of Millwall fans wrecked a pub in the high street, and another small mob fought with police at Pier Hill. A massive police presence ensured that the game itself was fairly peaceful, but later that night a mob of 60 Millwall fans smashed up a pub on the seafront, putting every window through and attacking a policeman with bottles and ashtrays. In all, 118 people were arrested and although not all were Millwall fans, the latter had hardly endeared themselves to the local population.

Back at The Den, things were still on a downward spiral. In 1980, a lump of concrete thrown from the terraces hit a linesman during the game against Shrewsbury, and the fans were involved in incidents throughout the country as they battled their way through the Third Division. In 1982 things took yet another turn for the worse. During an FA Cup tie against Slough Town, Millwall fans went on the rampage and fought with local fans as well as, it was rumoured, Chelsea supporters. The Millwall chairman went ballistic and threatened to close down the club if the fans' behaviour did not improve. The rest of that season was relatively quiet, but 1984 was to see the beginning of a steady rise in the number of incidents and a sharp increase in the number of high-profile ones.

The first of these took place on the night of a Milk Cup tie against their old foes, Chelsea. The West London club brought thousands to The Den and proceeded to swamp the area, in their favoured tactic. A concerted police action drove numerous pockets of fans from both clubs out of the sidestreets, but eventually everyone ended up in the Old Kent Road, resulting in a massive off. Many people were injured, almost all by flying glass, as the police somehow managed to keep the fans apart. In the end, the home supporters managed to keep on top, and as far as they were concerned, the pattern was set. With trouble at football on the increase throughout the country and numerous mobs on the rise, the Millwall fans decided that if they were to enhance their reputation even further, they would have to go for it in a big way. Seeing off challenges from the likes of Chelsea was an essential part of that process.

The next incident involved another club Millwall were familiar with, Bristol City. City had always been a bit of a thorn in the side of the East End club because they were one of the few sets of supporters not afraid to have a go, either at home or away. The feud had started the season before, when City came to London and their fans wrecked one of the Millwall pubs. This led to the Millwall supporters exacting revenge when they next travelled to Bristol. They began this as soon as they got off the train, wrecking a pub three miles from the ground, then launched a series of ambushes and attacks on Bristol City's pubs. A number of Bristol fans were stabbed, while another suffered a broken back after a frenzied assault. The City fans then began to go on the offensive, mobbing-up and attacking Millwall supporters wherever they found them. Two Millwall fans were seized and thrown over a railway bridge; many more were attacked and suffered serious injuries. Inside the stadium, the situation was manic. The Millwall fans had infiltrated almost every part of the ground and trouble erupted almost immediately, before the police somehow managed to gain control.

A few weeks later, the City fans decided to take their own revenge for the broken back suffered by one of their number, and planned an attack on one of the Millwall firm's pubs. The Bristol pub that had been wrecked by Millwall next to the station had a huge wooden sign outside, and this was 'liberated' by the City fans and taken to London the next time Millwall were at home. The City fans then sprayed 'BCFC' on it in red paint and at half-past two, with the Millwall pub packed out, they pulled up outside and threw it through the pub window before doing the off. The Millwall fans were furious and decided that they would finish this once and for all.

When it came, the attack was almost unprecedented. The next time Bristol City travelled to The Den, their supporters' coaches were directed down a dead-end nine miles from the ground and totalled by a huge mob of Millwall supporters, using all sorts of missiles and weaponry. Everyone at both clubs was astonished at the ferocity of the attack, while the police were furious that they had been unaware of anything being planned. However, the fans weren't finished yet because worse was only a matter of months way. Millwall fans were soon to be involved in what has become not only one of the most infamous episodes in hooligan history, but also a turning point for football fans everywhere.

In March 1985, the Millwall fans travelled to Kenilworth Road for an FA Cup quarter-final tie against L*t*n. The club took thousands to this match and this led to many of the problems on the night as the police, already on full alert, were taken aback at the excessive numbers. The fans had already been involved in numerous incidents in the town, but the police forced them up and into the ground as quickly as they could. The problems inside began as the Millwall fans were crammed into the away enclosure which was clearly too small for them. Just after the start they spilled out onto the pitch, delaying the game for 25 minutes. Once the match restarted, a number of fights broke out in various parts of the ground but were soon dealt with by an increasingly nervous police force. With Millwall losing 1–0 and only ten minutes to go, several hundred fans spilled onto the touchline in an attempt to force the abandonment of the game. They forced their way through the police cordon onto the pitch but were repelled twice before the referee, himself a police inspector and determined to finish the game, blew for full-time. As soon as the whistle went, the Millwall fans flooded onto the pitch. The police had no chance.

The fans went for the seated enclosure, ripped out seats and attacked the police with them. The police then regrouped and baton-charged the Millwall fans, who first pulled back and then attacked again. Other Millwall fans poured onto the pitch and astonishing scenes took place as the police, stewards and Millwall fans fought for control of the pitch. Eventually the Millwall fans began to calm down, but as they were driven out of the ground they kicked things off again, causing untold damage to houses and cars outside the stadium and wrecking the train taking them back to London. It was an episode that left 47 people, including 31 policemen, injured.

Football was shocked and the very next day, UEFA awarded Euro 88 to Germany, something the FA attributed directly to the L*t*n riot. However, of more importance was the fact that the violence had been screened on television and the entire country had watched open-mouthed as the events unfolded before their very eyes. That did it as far as the government were concerned, and Mrs Thatcher made it clear to the FA that if they did not sort things out, she would. The FA, reeling from this, hit the club with a £7,500 fine and made all the following season's Cup ties involving Millwall all-ticket affairs. For the hooligans, though, it was simply a massive result as they had shown everyone what they were capable of and they continued their activities. There was more trouble at Southampton and also at The Den, where seventeen fans were arrested and five injured during fighting when Millwall played Leeds United.

With the club now under attack from all sides, the fans continued on their path of destruction. In 1986, a football fan was stabbed by Millwall supporters during an attack at Charing Cross, and in Hove they caused mayhem before the Brighton game, smashing windows and fighting with local youths in Hove Park. Indeed, following that game, a small mob travelled to Eastbourne where they ran riot in the town's nightclub area, smashing windows, fighting with locals and wrecking a pub. Later that season, a group of about 40 Millwall fans staged a daring attack on a train carrying Charlton fans at New Cross station. They used bottles, bricks and even benches during the assault, as they attempted to fight their way onto the train to get at the opposing fans.

By now, in the post-L*t*n, Bradford and Heysel era, football was under intense scrutiny, with Millwall in particular under the watchful eye of the FA. As a result, things calmed down a little and the number of major incidents began to decline. Yet the hooligans still played up on their travels and it was clear that something more radical would have to be done. The key was to come up with the right idea – but sadly the matter was resolved for Millwall in 1989 by events at Hillsborough. As a result of the tragedy and the subsequent Taylor Report, the club decided that they would have to move to a new ground if they were ever to comply with all of the recommendations. When this was announced, fans everywhere let out a collective sigh of relief at the thought of the walk to The Den being no more. However, another three seasons would pass before the move was completed, which left plenty of opportunity to play up in the old spiritual home. In November 1990, the Millwall fans did battle with their local rivals West Ham in what the local police described as 'a flashback to the seventies'. Four hundred fans fought with each other outside the ground, damaging property and injuring a number of policemen before order was restored. In 1992, the Arsenal striker Ian Wright was hit by a coin thrown from the Millwall enclosure at Highbury during a Coca-Cola Cup tie, and in the second leg his team-mate Nigel Winterburn suffered the same fate. In the following January, the Millwall fans went to Southend for an FA Cup tie and again caused mayhem, resulting in 20 arrests.

The last ever game at The Den in May 1993 was always going to be an emotional occasion, but the club were ill-prepared for the events that unfolded as the team took to the field against Bristol Rovers. The longer the game went on, the more problems there were in the stands, with supporters tearing out seats and eventually invading the pitch. They then began ripping up the pitch and causing severe damage to the ground. In the end, it all degenerated into ugly scenes which did a major disservice to *all* of those linked with the club. It was a deplorable episode even by Millwall's standards.

The club now took up residence at the New Den and set out on the new season in optimistic mood. However, things didn't start very well as the fans went for it again in September, when severe crowd trouble erupted at The Valley. Police were forced to separate fighting mobs inside the ground and made ten arrests, while the Charlton chairman was attacked by a fan supposedly from Millwall. More fighting erupted outside the ground as Charlton fans, furious at the events inside, fought back. This incident caused dismay at Millwall. Having moved into the smart new all-seater ground only weeks before, they were convinced that they had created an environment to calm the fighting hordes, yet this episode had made it abundantly clear that little had changed. It certainly made many at the club wonder if it was all really worth it. However, on the pitch at least, the season was finishing on a high. The team reached the play-offs and were all set to entertain Derby County at the New Den.

Such was the importance of this game, the police made it known that they would be all over the fans to ensure that things went peacefully – but the increasingly organised violence associated with the football mobs saw the two sets of fans indulge in a massive off in Rotherhithe more than an hour before kick-off. Police called in reinforcements to calm things down, but this was only a prelude to the events surrounding the game.

DERBY

I have to say that in all my years following Derby, I have never experienced anything like that game at Millwall. Outside was bad enough but once the game was underway, it was ridiculous. We all know Derby are no angels and certainly have a mob who look for trouble, but those lot . . . mental. Totally mad. When the game started, the black players on our side were just given so much racial abuse it was disgusting. I really thought that we had seen the last of all that, but these lot were really having a go. It was obviously getting to our players, especially Paul Williams who looked a bit shaky. Well, they were everywhere, fighting and giving out abuse, it was really scary. Near the end, when we knew that we'd won, we were all going mad but it was obvious that they were going to go on the pitch. I just didn't expect to see what I saw.

Just before the end, the two black lads were substituted, more for their own safety than anything else, but once the whistle went, the Millwall fans came flooding on. I saw one of them punch our keeper in the mouth, and then another load attacked Mark Pembridge as he ran off. How they all got off I'll never know, it was outrageous.

After the game, we were scared shitless. They were everywhere outside and were really looking for us. The police kept us in for ages but managed to get us on the coaches without much happening. We knew, though, that they would attack them and they did, even though we turned the lights off and closed the curtains. Bricks were bouncing off the windows within a couple of minutes, but we got out okay. I won't go back there though, ever. They were mental. Even women stood on the doorsteps were giving us two fingers.

This was an extraordinary incident. At the pre-arranged off at Rotherhithe, both sets of fans were using mobile phones to call up reinforcements before the police could get there. There were also groups attempting to ambush coaches carrying Derby fans as they came into London, while others were hiding in a council estate that they knew the Derby fans would have to cross. Similarly, after the game the Millwall fans rampaged through the car park for over 90 minutes, rolled a Radio Derby car onto its roof, and fought with riot police. They then moved away from the ground into the tube, where fighting erupted again as Derby fans attempted to get away from East London. The FA immediately charged the club with failing to control its supporters and eventually hit them with a £100,000 fine, docked them three points and ordered them to play two matches behind closed doors. Incredibly, in spite of the history of trouble involving the fans, the FA suspended this punishment for three years.

The Millwall supporters were themselves coming under increasing attack from the fighting firms of other clubs, who saw them as not only fair game but prime targets as they sought to boost their own reputations. In 1994 there was a good example of this when Stoke City supporters smashed up and then fire-bombed two pubs in the Old Kent Road frequented by Millwall fans. It is fair to say that by this time, the Millwall supporters, although still highly active on the hooligan front, were no longer the force they once were. The declining (playing) fortunes of the club together with the advancing ages of many of the more volatile fans, saw their number of active hooligans markedly decrease. However, the undercurrent of hooliganism remained with the club and it surfaced again the following season when they were drawn to play Chelsea at the New Den in the FA Cup.

As we saw in the Chelsea section, there is no doubt that their supporters came in force and were determined to take over Millwall. Trouble began early on the Saturday morning as fans fought on the underground and in local pubs, but inside the ground it erupted just after the start of the second half when Chelsea supporters who had infiltrated the home fans began chanting and dishing out abuse. This led to a number of minor offs, but near the end of the game, Chelsea supporters in the away end began a concerted effort to get at the home fans, who responded with fists, boots and flying seats. With the game drawn, the replay at Stamford Bridge was always going to be emotive. Again fighting erupted before the game, but it was clear that the trouble at Millwall had stopped many of the East End fans from travelling. While the game was actually underway things remained quite calm, but once it went into extra-time matters got progressively worse. An attempted pitch-invasion by the Chelsea fans was averted by the police, but they were soon under attack from the fans who were using seats as missiles. Then things really turned nasty when Chelsea's John Spencer missed his penalty to hand the tie to Millwall. The Chelsea fans poured onto the pitch and attacked two Millwall players, and with the pitch covered in furious Chelsea fans, it took mounted police to keep them away from the Millwall end. Large-scale violence was avoided by this police action, but outside things went from bad to worse as fans fought with bottles, bricks and missiles. The Millwall fans also used CS gas in an attack against the police and at the end of it all, 20 policemen were left injured and 33 supporters had been arrested. The FA, again, were outraged, but this time it was Chelsea who took the blame and not just from the football authorities: the Chelsea chairman congratulated the Millwall fans in the stadium on their behaviour in the face of extreme provocation.

From that point onwards, the large-scale problems associated with the club began to decline, resurfacing only sporadically. The excellent work done by the club following the move to the New Den was beginning to pay dividends, as increasing numbers of family supporters were attracted back to their local club. On their travels it was often a different storm as the aggressive attentions of the police usually ensured that the mood among the Millwall fans soon became an ugly one, and when things happened, they usually found their way into the papers. In August 1995, Millwall travelled to Reading, itself a club with a small but hostile following, and after the almost obligatory trouble before the match, things really got nasty when an 8½-inch spanner was thrown at, and narrowly missed, the Reading keeper. The police went crazy and made a nasty situation inside the ground even worse as they sought to arrest the individual responsible. The following day, the FA were furious and the papers were full of it, calling this yet another new low in the history of the club. Later that same season, a Millwall fan got onto the pitch and threatened the Sheffield Wednesday keeper Kevin Pressman, in full view of the television cameras. With many saying that it was only a matter of time before a player was seriously injured by a supporter getting on the pitch with a weapon, there was talk of bringing back the fences. Thankfully, that came to nothing.

The reputation of the fans, although in decline following their relatively trouble-free recent history, still made them an attractive target for opposing firms and in April 1996, Stoke City supporters decided that they would attempt to turn the club over big-style. By all accounts, they put together a massive mob of around

300–400, with the idea that most of them would meet up and travel with the main bulk of fans while others would travel independently. However, the police had received information on their plans and arrested 25 known Stoke City hooligans in Dundee and another 20 in Cheltenham as they set out to travel to the game. They also managed to separate another 160 members of the Stoke firm from the main bulk of the support and kept them under close observation. The plan worked, but outside the ground, the Millwall fans, frustrated at the lack of opportunity to take these interlopers on, mobbed up and threw missiles at the 300 policemen on duty, seriously injuring a mounted officer and his horse.

At the end of that same season, Millwall went to Ipswich for the final game staring relegation in the face after a spectacular run of poor results. Some 2,500 travelled with the club and trouble erupted early on the morning of the game, as Millwall fans began to arrive in the Suffolk town.

The police, staging a massive operation to deal with the anticipated trouble if the club were relegated, attempted to keep the Millwall supporters in specific pubs, but this plan failed as the fans came into the town from all directions in a concerted show of strength. A 0–0 draw, and results elsewhere, left the club in the relegation zone and the fans went for it big-style, ripping up seats in the ground and hurling them at the police and rival fans. Despite the presence of 200 police and security guards around the pitch, the home side's end-of-season lap of honour was prevented, which caused more problems among the Ipswich supporters. When the Millwall fans were eventually let out of the ground, they clashed with rival supporters and again with the police, who by this time were in full riot gear. The trouble continued as the Millwall fans were escorted to the railway station and at least seventeen of them were arrested.

With the club now in the Second Division, the activities of the fans received little or no attention from the media. However, things were far from over and the reduction in overall support meant that the hard-core formed a larger percentage of the travelling fans. For the police, this should have meant that they were easier to control, but that was not always the case as events at various clubs were to prove.

This is, of course, merely a brief history of the club's notorious supporters and it is fair to say that almost every time they travel away, things will happen. They have long-standing rivalries with numerous other clubs, but in particular with Portsmouth, Birmingham (which we will look at later) and West Ham. Indeed, Millwall's East London rivals have been at the forefront of their attentions over the years (in one incident at Surrey Quays station they were ambushed by a mob of Millwall fans 'armed' with pitbull terriers) and as far as Portsmouth are concerned, the list of incidents is endless. There have been attacks at Waterloo station involving almost 200 rival fans, and mobs of Millwall terrorising shoppers in Portsmouth city centre. More bizarrely, during one of Millwall's enforced absences from The Den, the club were forced to play their games at Fratton Park, which meant that every time they played there, the two sets of fans would have it away. One such, particularly violent, episode took place in 1978 and involved not only Millwall and Pompey but also Bristol Rovers and the newly formed Anti-Nazi League, who were intent on taking on the East London supporters. The city was overrun with people intent on fighting and it took a massive effort to keep them apart, one that only partly succeeded as a number of pubs were wrecked. Yet another crazy incident involving the Millwall fans took place at Reading when, following a 4–0 defeat, they began attacking Reading fans outside the ground. As they moved down into the town they began baiting groups of black youths, who themselves mobbed-up and attacked the Millwall fans with missiles and wooden stakes. This fighting continued for over 40 minutes before the police could get a grip of it and severe damage had been caused to property in the town centre by the time the Millwall fans left. They were also implicated in a brutal attack on a man on a moped who was studying 'The Knowledge'. He stumbled across the Millwall fans while wearing an Arsenal shirt, for which he was dragged off his bike and slashed with a knife. When he called for help, another group of Millwall fans came over and gave him another beating for exactly the same reason.

CAPITAL PUNISHMENT

It is important to stress that what we are talking about at Millwall is a minority of supporters, but it is also necessary to remember that it is a sizeable and very vocal minority. The financial problems associated with the club since early 1997 have caused severe unrest among the club's supporters in general, but the hooligan elements have been the ones who have responded more vehemently. The pitch invasion and subsequent trouble surrounding the Bristol City game at the New Den in February 1997 was evidence of this. These East London fans have always been regarded as among the worst-behaved in football, and that is a label they richly deserve. They have systematically taken violence around the Football League with them, and it is astonishing that they have been able to continue almost unchecked for so long. The FA, while happy to hand out fines and ground closures, have never attempted anything remotely aimed at changing the attitudes of the fans, and have left it up to the police and the club itself to control. Time will tell whether the club can sort out its financial problems, but if the evidence of its failure with its hooligan following is anything to go by, it is in severe trouble.

Chapter 8
The Bushwhackers

Like most football clubs with an active hooligan following, Millwall found itself with an organised mob very early on. Indeed, it is felt by many that Millwall's were the first 'named' firms in English football, and those were of course the 'Half-Way Liners', 'Treatment' and the infamous 'F-Troop'.

All of these groups came to prominence in the mid-seventies but were immortalised in the 1977 *Panorama* documentary which took their exploits into the living-rooms of the British public. It described how the Half-Way Liners were younger kids, usually under fourteen, whose job it was to wind-up the opposing fans and scout out where they were and what pubs they were in, primarily when they came to the East End. From there, these youngsters graduated to Treatment, notorious for their chanting and the habit of wearing surgical headgear on the terraces. Many fans believe that this form of costume was adopted purely for the benefit of the TV cameras, but if it were the norm then this bizarre 'uniform' is unique among football fans because it is the only time we are aware of that a firm has worn clothing designed to make them stand out (the idea usually being to blend into the background and avoid detection, either by the police or the opposing fans). It may seem almost comical now, but back in the seventies the sight of a mob of blokes wearing these light-blue hats would put the fear of God into the rival supporters. After a spell with Treatment, the would-be hooligans progressed to F-Troop. Named after a popular television programme of the time and renowned for being totally fearless and very violent, it was this group's activities that took Millwall's already-bad reputation and made it one of the worst in football. They travelled to every game, home or away, and caused as much trouble as possible, particularly up north where they usually made great play of the north–south divide. They were also involved in making the walk to The Den one of the most feared in football. Intimidation on a scale unknown at any other football ground was in evidence at Cold Blow Lane, and countless people were attacked and severely beaten over the years simply for daring to visit the club to support the opposing team.

By the late seventies and early eighties, the three firms had all but merged into the now-infamous 'Bushwhackers', formed primarily as a show of solidarity against the police (far better to have a single large gang than a number of smaller ones). They were soon regarded by many of the Millwall fans as an integral part of the culture surrounding the club, and wasted no time in letting the rest of football know they were out and about. They set out at the start of the 1980–81 season with the intention of re-establishing themselves as *the* top boys.

Their activities soon attracted the attention of right-wing organisations such as the National Front and, in a traditionally insular area, the political parties had some measure of success. However, they never made the inroads at Millwall (nor at West Ham, for that matter) that they did at Chelsea, for the simple reason that the East End has always had a strong mix of ethnic groups and, even at this early stage, the Bushwhackers had a number of members who were black. (As proof of this, if you study the footage of the L*t*n riot, almost half the faces on the pitch are coloured.) The East London football fans always saw the club as far more important than anything else, and regarded all those who supported it with them as part of one big 'family', so black Millwall fans were welcomed.

For the Millwall firm, the favoured tactic was always intimidation. This was assisted by the fact that the mere mention of the club sent (and sends?) shivers down the spine. The fact that no one knew what they would do next on their travels was perhaps the most worrying thing, but at home things were even worse because they had the ability to vanish if the need arose. The tube network was always a favourite battleground for the fans; New Cross, London Bridge and Surrey Quays have all seen spectacular battles involving Millwall, but they would also venture further afield, even up into North London, for battles with their rivals.

The drive to be the 'top boys' continued for the next five seasons, culminating in the now-famous attack on the Bristol City coaches when the Bushwhackers took the hooligan issue to a new level and confirmed the existence of organised football violence to what had been a sceptical media. Just a year later, the L*t*n riot saw the group achieve almost cult status among hooligan groups for the sheer ferocity of their assault not just on the opposing fans but also on the police. The response and condemnation it provoked placed the Bushwhackers at the forefront of police investigations and the FA anti-hooligan initiatives. Despite this, the mob continued to spread its violence. In 1986, they set out for the West Bromwich Albion fixture with only one thing on the agenda: revenge. Earlier that year, a Millwall fan had been killed during a fight in Sheffield's Arndale Gate. He had actually died when he hit his head after missing a drop-kick aimed at a local youth and fractured his skull, but the Bushwhackers saw this as an attack on them and had made repeated threats to supporters of both Sheffield United and Wednesday. Following the West Brom game, the mob travelled into Birmingham where they hired a number of minibuses and vans and set off for Sheffield. When they arrived, they moved to The Royal, one of the well-known pubs in the area, and began drinking and being generally abusive. A fight ensued and the landlord called the police, but by the time they arrived, 40 people were fighting in the street outside and the police were forced to call for reinforcements. The situation deteriorated and the fights turned into running battles involving upwards of 70 people. It took the police some considerable time to regain control and eventually they arrested seventeen people, most of them from London, and recovered weapons including flick-knives, razor-knives and a broken snooker-cue. For the Bushwhackers, the point had been made and revenge had been exacted.

The Millwall fans had long been under investigation not just by the Metropolitan Police but also by the British Transport Police. Undercover operations had been mounted against the group and four of the alleged ringleaders were jailed in the early eighties for their part in organised football violence. However, the collapse of Operation 'Own-Goal' saw all outstanding charges against Millwall fans dropped and the four alleged members of the Bushwhackers had their sentences cut on appeal on 17 October 1989. Despite this, the police continued to mount operations against the Millwall fans and although very few arrests were ever made, there can be no doubt that numerous incidents were averted as a result of these actions.

By the early nineties, it was widely perceived that the Bush-whackers *were* the Millwall travelling support, and thus the treatment of the 'average' Millwall football fan, never the best anyway, began to deteriorate. Police forces and stewards around the country had always been wary of the club's fans and it is fair to say that they were often wound up to expect trouble from them. Of course, over-aggressive policing itself *did* lead to the fans responding violently, but attitudes were changing at the club and a number of complaints were made to the FA about the treatment handed out to their fans. For the Bushwhackers themselves, things progressed as normal. The Taylor Report and the use of CCTV had been instrumental in driving them out of grounds, but they still played up whenever they had the opportunity – and if that was on their travels, then more often than not the local police were happy merely to get rid of them rather than detain them. For the police, the main difficulty centred on the fact that the members of the firm were invariably older than they were used to. (While the 'average hooligan' has always been perceived as being in his late teens or early twenties, the Bushwhackers and the other top London firms, are renowned for being significantly older, with many in their mid-thirties and even forties. This in itself has been sufficient to scare the shit out of many fighting groups around the country who have been unable to handle this concept.)

The move to the New Den was supposed to be a turning point for both the firm and the club. The run-down nature of the old ground in Cold Blow Lane had often been cited as a reason for the fans' behaviour, and the superb facilities at the new ground – including, of all things, a creche – were designed to remove the intimidating atmosphere so prevalent at the 'Old Den'. However, following the trouble at the final game at Cold Blow Lane, it quickly became clear that the atmosphere at the New Den could be just as intimidating. Certainly the walk to the ground, one way in and one way out past all the rubbish and derelict land, was just as bad. Nevertheless, things did go well at the New Den until the play-off game against Derby when the violence reached a new low. Players being substituted to protect them from racist abuse and others being attacked by fans were things that had not been seen at the club for a number of years, and it sent shock-waves through the game. Yet despite this, the Bushwhackers have continued their activities almost unchecked, though not without some degree of humour. Pre-season friendlies had usually seen the club take the team up to Scotland and with them had gone a small band of supporters. The history surrounding the club of course made these supporters totally unwelcome, so they devised a number of ingenious methods to hide their identity. One of the more famous was styling themselves as the *Bermondsey Male-Voice Choir* (a group of gentlemen who did little singing but lots of drinking), although latterly, 30 members of the Combined Union of Tree Surgeons (CUNTS), approved by a number of local authorities according to their booking applications, have also joined this growing throng.

However, it would not do to make light of their activities because they are a vicious group intent on violence. The fact that they have been allowed to continue almost unhindered for so long is worrying, but of equal concern is the fact that the declining fortunes of the club will provide an excuse for them to become even more active. The club does not seem able to deal with them and nor do the police, but it is clear to supporters everywhere that something must be done if football at the New Den is ever to achieve the level of safety that the ground, and the true, non-violent supporters, truly deserve.

For almost every football hooligan, the main match in the season is the local derby fixture. This is the one club that you hate more than any other and it's bred into you from day one; you *must* hate *them*, it's traditional.

Unfortunately, with football being the way it is, you don't always get to meet the team you hate most and this can lead to other rivalries starting up, which grow and grow until they become almost (but not quite) as important. Two clubs that share such a rivalry are Millwall and Birmingham City. Both clubs have a large, active and renowned hooligan following and the two firms hate each other with a passion. For one to lose face to the other would be hard to live down, so whenever the two meet, violence is sure to be close at hand. Below, supporters from both clubs describe the way in which the hatred has often manifested itself as open warfare, involving the organisation of violence on a scale that would frighten the life out of Joe Public.

THE LION AND THE ZULU

Birmingham:
Like London, we in the Midlands have our share of derby games and there are clubs around here with some well-handy firms, the Bridge Boys (Wolves), the Naughty Forty (Stoke), Section Five (West Brom) and the Baby Squad (Leicester). Everyone in the country knows about City's Zulu Army – we'll take on anyone and run from no one. The derby games give us plenty of action, but going to London is different altogether and taking on the Cockneys always makes days away in the capital that little bit special.

I think that we are one of the few clubs that take big numbers of lads down to London no matter who we are playing. We do that because they expect it of us now, and you never know who you are going to come across. For one of the London clubs to put it out that they turned over the Zulus would really give their reputation something. They know we are one of, if not *the*, top firms in the country and we have proved that by taking it to the capital over and over. The London firms are naughty, there is no doubt about that, and you know that the top three will show if it's been sorted out – but contrary to what they like to think, there are plenty of firms around the country that would tear them apart. The mouthy Cockney Wanker has been sent packing many a time, once he ventures out of the M25, along with his blade.

Us and Millwall have had this thing going for a good few years now, which I remember as starting around 1985. We hadn't played them for a while, so the visit to The Den was one of the top games that season. At that time they were well at it, and we knew this away-day would mean a lot to the firms from both clubs. We had kept the whole thing as quiet as possible, as we wanted to take their lads by surprise. Small mobs made their way to the meeting-place in groups of anything from five to 30, and once we were all firmed-up we totalled around 400. There was no way this lot were going to get legged, they were all top lads with the bottle to see it off, and every one of them was mad for getting down to Millwall. What a feeling that is, being part of something that could at any minute throw a place into chaos; enough to make the hair on your neck stand up.

We made our way across London to New Cross with no police in sight. When we came out of the station, the police couldn't believe what had arrived. Neither could the young lads who took it upon themselves to act as spotters. They hadn't seen anything like this before. This wasn't just ten lads trying to look as though they were going shopping, lads they could finger to the locals in the pubs. We wanted it big-time, and they were soon on their toes. We made our way to the ground passing every pub, waiting for the off. We were all over the road, putting on a major show. There we were, taking fucking liberties at Millwall. The locals must have had it away, because we saw nothing but the odd small group down side-roads. The buzz was banging away. It's amazing to think that you can get that many lads across London without anyone finding out, but it wasn't the first time and wouldn't be the last. The police finally got hold of it after coming in from every direction and got us to the ground as quick as possible. During the game, the atmosphere was like an anti-climax. You still couldn't really spot the Millwall firm and they were well quiet. After the game, we were taken by the police all the way back to Euston with no hassle. It's a fantastic feeling when you go to a place, take the piss and know that every firm in the country will find out what happened within a few weeks.

Millwall:

When they first came down it really did take us by surprise. We had expected something, but nothing like the firm they brought. No one from outside London had ever tried that on before and, really, they took the piss. I have to hand it to them for what they did, but a lot of our lads were well angry and thought it was bollocks, a cop-out. It fucked them off that Birmingham didn't let us know they were coming so that we could have met up to really have it away. They didn't turn any of the pubs over or nothing, so really it ended up being all show. But credit where credit's due, it was some show and it was one tasty firm. After the game, the place was crawling with Old Bill so all we could do was pick out the odd car-load. After something like that, anyone is fair game; I mean, you can't let them take liberties like that without any payback.

The next season, the first meeting was again down here at The Den. It was a night match and right at the start of the season. For Millwall, this had to be payback time. There was no way they would get that many blokes down here again without getting spotted, so we were out all day covering Euston, King's Cross and St Pancras. The police were also more than ready for them this time. The Met knew the locals were out for it and were popping up everywhere we went, trying to break up any group they could spot. It was bollocks – this time, if they were coming, it wasn't going to be by train, so we decided to head down to London Bridge as the police usually pick up the coaches around there before bringing them in. There were plenty of Millwall waiting but all we saw was the mums and dads' coaches. While we were wasting our time, the real action was taking place much closer to home.

Birmingham:
As this was a night game, we were never going to get the same crew as last time. Going by train would have been a complete waste because we knew Millwall would be all over town and we just wouldn't have the numbers. So we hired our own coach and 40 of us made our way down.

As the driver got near to London Bridge, he told us that he had to contact the police so that we could be escorted in. Fuck that, being escorted in meant no trouble and we hadn't come down for nothing. It would have also made us look like we had bottled out and with 40 lads breathing down his neck he couldn't really refuse, and so we soon moved off down towards the ground. A lot of the lads had come well tooled-up, which was another reason for not wanting to attract the police. As we approached a pub near the ground, we could see all these Millwall drinking outside. As we went past they clocked us, and looking out the back window you could see more starting to pile out. Then about another 50 yards down the road, we passed another pub rammed with more lads. We were well outnumbered by now and could see them mobbing-up and starting to come down the road after us. The bus driver, not really knowing what was going on, then stopped the bus as we got held up in traffic. As soon as the Millwall seen this, they started to steam down after us. There were about 200 of them and they were well tooled-up and going mental. They put through all the windows and were trying to drag people off the bus. The driver got the bus out and off to the ground as quick as possible, thank fuck. Inside the bus we found bricks, bits of metal, glasses and milk crates. It was fucking mad; scary as fuck but kind of funny at the same time. Even after something like that, some of the lads were wanting to go back and have a go. The police seemed to find the whole thing funny; I think they thought we deserved a hiding after making them look wankers the year before. I think they also thought it would stop us from coming down again. Would it fuck!

We didn't play Millwall again for a few seasons due to being in different divisions, but once we were up to meet them again, the old rivalries came back. Once again it was down to London and another pre-arranged meeting-place, but different from the one we had used before. This time Millwall were made aware that we would be coming, but to our surprise we made it to New Cross without any police or Millwall showing. In total we had 250 to 300 lads – not easy to miss, but we made it. The police had got word we were on the tube, and were ready to take us from the station to the ground. It was only then that we started to see the Millwall lads, who were looking mighty pissed-off as the police kept us both well apart. Once again we had come and taken the piss. The police announced that they were laying on a special train to take us back to Euston after the match. Out of that mob, about half of us decided to take this train and I was one of them; the others wanted to make their own way in the hope that something might still go off. I made the wrong decision.

Millwall:
The next time they came down saw the major off at London Bridge. We had waited for these bastards for a few seasons, but all the information we were given before the game proved to be bollocks. We were out looking for coaches and scouting at Moorgate, but they must have changed their

meet because once again they came all the way without getting turned over. They must have thought they were the dog's bollocks coming down and taking the piss again, but our main plan was to ambush them on the way back at London Bridge. They had a good turn-out, but during the match we were told that the Old Bill were going to get all their lads back up to Euston on a special, which really would have fucked everything.

After the match we got the nod that most of their lads were still looking for it, trying to break away from the escort and making their own way. They did have the bottle for it all right, so we left them and all made our way to the meet just around the corner from London Bridge station. By the time I arrived, there were about 200 Millwall waiting, all tooled-up. Within ten minutes that number had doubled. Word came back that the Brummies had arrived, so some of the top lads went around in a car to let them know we were waiting.

Birmingham:
Me and a few of the lads were drinking up at Euston, checking out what was going on and waiting to catch up with some of the lads that made their own way, to find out if anything had kicked off. Eventually some of the lads turned up and told us what we had missed. They told us that the Millwall were nowhere to be seen after the game, so the police numbers had dropped off once they got to London Bridge. Our lot were hanging around in the hope that it would happen, when this car pulled up and told them that the Millwall were waiting down this side-road. We still had a fair firm, so once they grouped together the lads moved off, leaving the police who didn't have a clue. Once they got in the road, the Millwall came steaming out from under this archway. They were well tooled-up and ran the Blues back up the steps and into the station. The lads then regrouped and armed themselves by ripping a newsagent's stand to pieces before charging back out and into the

Millwall lads outside. They did a runner back down the steps and our lads looked like getting back on top. Then there was a stand-off as the police made a show. Our lads were at the top of the steps, with the Millwall at the bottom, when from out of the Millwall firm came these ten or so blokes wearing gas masks. They moved up the steps then fired tear gas into our mob. The police just fucked off and the Blues lads ran back into the station. The Millwall then came into the station and legged our lads everywhere – some had even run down the tracks as trains were coming towards them, just to get away. Some of our lads were well pissed-off with us for not sticking together, because they felt that we could have turned the Millwall over on their own patch. They had still put on a good show – but the Millwall lads won the day.

The next time we met was our first visit to the New Den. Once again this was a big day out. The meeting-place was set, but was changed at the last minute. Unfortunately, we had travelled down by car and parked-up out of town to get the tube down, so we hadn't been told, along with a few others we met up with. The police up here knew we were taking big numbers down and they would have told the Met what to expect, so the top lads had changed plans. At that time we didn't have a clue as to why we were the only ones at the meet, which put the shits up us a bit, so we decided to go our separate ways rather than travel down as a small mob because that could have proved really dangerous, as well as getting us picked up.

As we were walking up the ramp at London Bridge, we saw this massive firm of around 300 coming out of the station. We were very nearly on our toes before we realised that they were all Blues! What a relief that was, and the police were nowhere to be seen. We joined the mob and almost everyone was tooled-up and really pumping. The ambush with the tear gas meant that we really had to get some payback, and these lads were banging for it. The plan was to head back to the archways and see if the Millwall were waiting again. There were two pubs on the corner of the road and we expected the Millwall to be mobbed-up inside. First a group of lads steamed the doors open of one and then the other, but the Millwall were not at home. To calm the nerves, we stopped for a drink before moving off down the Old Kent Road. That landlord must have been the luckiest bloke in London that day. If there had been even five or six local lads in there, his pub would have been finished. As it was, he took more money in about half an hour than he would have in the rest of the week. Once again a massive Blues firm marched into Millwall and the locals were nowhere. The police got hold of us about half a mile from the ground and escorted us in. As we got closer, little mobs started to appear and check out the numbers – but they were just mouthy wankers, we had taken the piss. After the game we expected the Millwall to really turn out. The police kept us in for ages, which should have given them the chance to sort themselves out, but as we marched back to Lewisham station all we saw were the little mobs. There was the odd bit of action as some Blues got out of the escort and chased them, but they were all well on their toes.

This time the police took us all the way back to Euston and seen us onto the train back home. They were all over us.

Millwall:
When they came to the New Den for the first time, they showed again in big numbers. But the Old Bill were all over the pubs and stations down here, and we couldn't get any kind of numbers together to go for it before the police came in and split us off into all directions. It was exactly the same after the match; they were kept in for ages while the police cleared us out. London Bridge was like a Filth reunion; no chance.

When we played them next it was at their gaff, we were top and they were second. The feeling down here was that they had got away with it once too often, so we really had to put on a show at their place. We got word from them that it was really up to us to show this time, and that they were well ready for us – and they were right. All the old faces were turning out for this one, it was back to the good old days. We went up by train, planning to stop on the edge of the city to get pissed-up and meet with other lads. Once we got near Birmingham, we were spotted by Old Bill on the train who stopped us, took all the beer as well as the names and escorted us to the ground. There were Brummies all over the place in little mobs, but nothing happened. When we arrived at the ground, we seen that the police had done exactly the same to all the buses by stopping them on the motorway. Some of the coaches had their windows put through and there were a lot of well pissed-off lads around. The team bus had been hit as well, bastards. We were just forced into the ground straight away.

Birmingham:
At fucking last, they showed at our place. The city was buzzing and the Zulu Army were everywhere you looked. The main hunting ground was around New Street station. We waited for the big mob to show, along with the police, but they only turned up in a little firm which the police took straight off to the ground. We heard that the coaches were being seen to, but that was mostly just the mums and that. Inside the ground was mental, what an atmosphere – pure hate and aggression. I wouldn't like to have been a player out there, because every time one came near the crowd he was spat on or had something thrown at him. The game was set off by two late goals, first by them to make it 2–1, then we equalised in the last two minutes. That was just what the police didn't want, because it had been going off in the corner for most of the match but if anyone in that crowd wasn't fired-up by then, they soon turned out to be. This was always going to go off, but the final whistle sent people onto the pitch and players running for safety. I was at the far end from the Millwall and everyone in that

stand couldn't wait to get out and have it away with the Cockneys. It was mad, we fucking hated them.

There were hundreds of Blues out looking for it. The police for some reason had let the Millwall out of the ground and were keeping them in the car park. That was just making it worse, because we could see them and they could see us. The police were really getting heavy in trying to get our lot away, which kicked it off. All this went on for over half an hour, then a lot of the lads started to move off and wait in the backstreets, as we found out that the police were thinking of closing New Street off until they were on their way south. The two firms were in contact with each other on the mobile phones, and the Millwall let our top lad know that they would try and break the police escort in Digbeth on the way to the station. We made our way to one of the pubs on the way and it was rammed. It seemed that everyone from years back had turned out, as well as all the lads that had been banned from matches. They can't keep you away all the time, and when it's in you, that's it.

We were getting a running commentary on what was happening over the phone by the lads that were watching the escort, and when they got close, we went out of the pub and I can honestly say that I've never seen Blues fans tooled-up like that. There was a transit van full of baseball bats, milk crates full of bottles, half-bricks, the lot. But loads of lads had the CS gas canisters, saying it was pay-back for the London Bridge off. We came out of the side-roads and there were Blues lads everywhere, all tooled-up. The Millwall had no chance of breaking out of the police escort as there were hundreds of police, horses, dogs, riot vans, and then the police helicopter came in overhead – all this for a football match. When you think about it, it's mad. They should have let us get on with it, it would have saved the taxpayer a fortune.

Millwall:
They had got us out of the ground to prevent us from ripping

the place apart and getting tooled-up, but then they kept us in the car park from where we could see the local lads giving it the large one. The locals finally fucked off and they moved us off to the station. They kept stopping every couple of hundred yards, which started to wind us up no end. Birmingham had plenty of boys out and the police were shitting it, although they did a good job of keeping us apart really, there was no way we were going to get at each other. I have never been in a situation like that before, it was like being at war. The police were getting busy with the locals and had closed off the main road up to the station. There was even a fucking helicopter doing the rounds. When we got up to the station they finally went for it as best they could, throwing bottles and stuff, but once that was done they really did a runner from the Old Bill who steamed into them. The coppers had cleared the station and they got us on the train and out of there as quick as they could. I must admit I hadn't seen anything like that before. There were a few lads that went back in that night and had it away, but the coppers really sorted that day out.

The return match at the New Den was billed as World War Three by the papers. Barry Fry was on the box saying he wouldn't bring his family and all that bollocks, and Birmingham were saying they didn't want anyone to travel. I think there were people from every club in London out on the tube that night, hoping to pick up a piece of the action, but in truth there were more press and camera crews than Brummies.

Birmingham:
After what happened at our place, the club said they wouldn't accept tickets for the match; but after pressure from the fans, they came up with this idea of selling a combined coach-and-match ticket for £21. I bought my ticket and was then told that I wouldn't receive my actual match-ticket until we were well on our way and after our last stop. I was having a beer by the ground before getting the coach

and there were plenty of lads saying that they were taking the train and would try to force the police into letting them in rather than having them roam around the tube.

As me and a fair few mates had already parted with our cash, we still went by coach. There were six coaches, taking about 250 all in all, and about 70 of those were lads. The police escorted us in from London Bridge and we were expecting the same sort of ambush as before, only this time the police had it all sorted. After the match, they got us out but we knew the Millwall were trying it on. Two windows on the coaches were put through, that's all.

Millwall:
They didn't bring many that night so we mainly had it away with the Old Bill, mostly out of frustration really. They did have more lads at Euston as they phoned to let our lads know, but apparently the Old Bill got hold and shipped them back north.

Birmingham:
There were well over 100 of our lads at Euston but the police were waiting for them. They were kept on three buses and assured that they were being escorted down to the match, once the police were certain that it was all of them. At eight o'clock, the police put them back on the train to Brum with an escort as far as Milton Keynes.

It is very interesting to note just how the tactics of the firms and the police change as such rivalries grow. There comes a time when turning up and putting on a show isn't enough, you must be seen to be seriously looking to get confrontation going. The firms will eventually be in contact and try to arrange a meet away from the watchful eye of the local constabulary, something that is becoming more and more common among the serious firms. As we have seen in this account, turning up unannounced, although respected, can sometimes be seen as a half-hearted challenge.

The police find meetings outside the capital much easier to

contain and will swamp an area, or one of the firms, in order to try to keep things under control. In London, the situation is much more difficult due to the size of the public transport system. As the police hold 50 lads at Kings Cross you can be sure that another little firm will have ducked back down the tube and given them the slip. Many meetings go unattended by the Met who will arrive just in time to clean up the mess. The police may at times appear to be well organised, but the hooligan will tell you that nine times out of ten it is more by luck than judgement that they achieve this.

PART FIVE
The Met

Chapter 9   *Police Action*
The Shed
The Hammer
Highbury
Bolton

Chapter 10   *Altogether Now*
Millwall, Brum, Rotterdam

Chapter 11   *European Links*
Unwelcome Visitors

Chapter 12   *Have The Hooligans Got It Sorted?*

Chapter 9
Police Action

The people with the job of keeping all these warring factions apart – not to mention dealing with those detained – are of course, the police, known universally in the capital as the 'Old Bill' or the 'Filth'. Whatever you think of them – and our opinions should be pretty clear by now – it is clear that they have a very important and, it has to be said, difficult role to play in this issue. While on many occasions they get it right, there are far too many where they get it completely wrong.

Back in the good old days of cobbled streets, leather balls and evil-looking hobnailed boots, football crowds could easily be policed by the local bobby and his dog. Although trouble existed, it was usually quite localised and in most cases the police presence was enough to deter anyone from doing anything they shouldn't. That was back in those distant days when the police were both respected and revered. Things began to change as more and more people, primarily young males, became involved in movements such as the Teddy Boys, the mods and the rockers and began rebelling against their parents, the police and society in general. This developed into violence, for example at seaside resorts, which eventually – and almost inevitably – found its way onto the football terraces. The above is all a bit simplistic, but nonetheless pretty accurate.

After England won the World Cup in 1966, the increasing

media interest in the game saw the newspapers take an unhealthy (or healthy, depending on your viewpoint) interest in hooliganism and it began to make frequent appearances on both the back and the front pages. This in itself caused problems because not only did it attract certain types of individuals to football, it also made those who frequented games more aware of the possible danger when they travelled and so they began to prepare for trouble. The general public demanded that the police get on top of the problem, and with violence on the up, their presence at grounds had to be increased.

Due to the early nature of the violence – i.e., irregular and spontaneous outbreaks – the police were always at least one or two steps behind those intent on fighting and their role was merely reactive. They could do little except try to judge which supporters were likely to cause trouble and flood the area with policemen in the hope that they could keep the hooligans apart. Within the confines of the capital, the police had a particularly difficult job due to the close proximity of the hooligan groups, which made the opportunities for confrontation all too frequent.

By the early seventies, the police had to a certain extent begun to get a grip of the problem within the stadia. However, outbreaks of violence on the terraces and pitch invasions were still regular occurrences throughout the country, and the police, by now almost battle-hardened to a Saturday at Upton Park, The Den or wherever, began to realise that they were on a losing wicket. The traditional respect for the London copper had all but vanished under the weight of the sixties' drive for so-called 'free expression', and they realised that if these hooligans wanted to fight then they would have to go down to their level and fight back. This attitude meant that things were not always done to the letter of the law, especially when severely provoked, as the following accounts seem to confirm.

THE SHED

Back in the early seventies, the coppers who worked at the Bridge, and certainly the ones who did the Shed, were complete arseholes. Don't get me wrong, back then Chelsea were mental and the police had a real job on their hands some days, especially when we were down in the Second Division. The thing was, back then, that the Chelsea lads even fought among themselves if there were no away fans. You had all the actual London lads at it with the mobs from outside London like Staines or Slough, all trying to become the top boys. Stupid really, because outside we always all came together.

I remember once, it was going mental up the Shed – just an off, no away fans – and the Bill were going frantic. They decided to send in the dogs to break things up and, as usual, as soon as the Old Bill moved in we would stop fighting each other and turn on them. Well, this time they let the dogs loose and they come in barking and snapping. There was a thing going on then that if you could take out a police dog you were made as far as everyone else was concerned, and this Alsatian gets the shit kicked out of it and thrown back over the fence. Well, I've never seen the coppers lose it like that. They came in beating the shit out of anyone that moved, nicking loads. There must have been about 20 taken out in all. Usually they kept you in the vans to cool down and then let you out, or if it was bad, drove you off and dumped you in another part of London. This time, though, after about 20 minutes this copper opens the door, points out me and these other two, then kicked the rest out.

We got taken off and I thought we were well fucked. After a few minutes, this copper turns round and says to us, 'Right, you bastards, you killed one of our police dogs and you lot are getting the kicking of your lives for it.' Two of them threw me in the back of a transit and kicked the shit out of me for about five minutes. I just curled up and took it. They threw me out on some waste ground, along with these other two, and just drove off. None of us were badly hurt. At the next home game, I saw one of the coppers but I don't think he remembered me. All the Chelsea kept making barking noises at them; that really fucked them off, that did.

THE HAMMER

I'd been travelling away with Spurs for a fair while and always hated going to Upton Park, because they can be mad down there. They were total animals back then, so you needed the numbers so you could at least have a go back. The Irons were bad enough on their own but the coppers . . . fuck me. They were like a second firm sometimes, they loved it. In all the time I ever went, I'd never known them to nick a home fan, it was amazing. Plenty of our lads ended up in court on the Monday but never any of theirs, and you saw plenty of them getting dragged out. Anyway, I once met up with this bloke who it turns out was an Iron, and as you do, we got to talking about football and fighting. Anyway, I asked him about all that with the law, and he told me that it was a sort of unwritten rule in the East End that the coppers wouldn't nick their own at football. A lot of the ones down at Upton Park were Irons through and through, and some would even kick things off. He even told me that there were a few that wore West Ham badges under the lapels on their jackets and would show them to the Hammers boys before it all went off. That way, the locals knew who they could follow in. Bastards.

HIGHBURY

It was the first time I'd been to London with Liverpool. There'd been loads of trouble, but inside the ground things were really bad because Arsenal had loads of lads in our end. The coppers, wankers, didn't seem that bothered, even though it was obvious who was who. Well, after about 20 minutes of the game, they kicked things off, our lot ran back up at them and things were getting really nasty. Being only young I wanted to keep out the way, but all the lads I was with started running up there and I didn't want to get left behind, so I went with them. All of a sudden, this copper appears in front of me and smacks me one right on the jaw. I just stood there seeing stars and my mates are all shouting at this copper, who then grabs me and drags me down onto the side of the pitch and out the ground. Before I know what's happening, I'm bundled in the back of a van with this fucking copper, all shitting myself thinking I am going to get a hiding as they shut the doors behind us. I pleaded innocence, but he just told me to 'Shut the fuck up, you Scouse cunt.' Well, like I say, I was only about fourteen, never in any trouble before and all I wanted was to get out of there. Thing was, he looked as shit-scared as me and there was only me and him there. After a couple of minutes, he just opened the door of the van and told me to fuck off. I was expecting at least a boot up the arse, but I never got it.

Now I don't know what makes coppers tick, but I reckon that copper dragged me out that ground because he was shitting it and his bottle had gone. He needed to get away and I was just the excuse he needed.

As the police began to fight back, segregation at football grounds was stringently enforced, not just in the capital but throughout Britain. They also began to use searches, early kick-offs and all-ticket games as weapons in the battle against hooliganism, but these made only a minor difference and following a particularly brutal season in 1976–77, the police, the football authorities and the government decided that enough was enough. The decision was taken to erect fencing around the pitches and on the terraces to keep the fans off the field and apart from each other.

Once the cages were up, the supporters became easier for the police to deal with. However, those intent on trouble would still find their way into the 'wrong' enclosure on occasions and when violence did erupt, it was now impossible for innocent supporters to get away quickly. Furthermore, the police often found it more difficult to get in and break things up, with the result that minor incidents quickly developed into major ones.

* * *

BOLTON

Bolton's a fucking shithole of a ground for away fans, if ever there was one. They are nasty bastards up there, with the numbers to back it up. Anyway, they scored and these lads started going mad in our section, obviously Bolton boys. The lads near them went right off, the full bollocks, and they were up against the fence trying to fight back. Everyone piled down and the sheer numbers meant that these lads got battered – and of course they couldn't get out. Their lot were going mad trying to get over the fences and come at us. Everything was going fucking crazy, you know what it used to be like.

Anyway, the coppers were trying to come in through the gates but our lads were forcing them shut and they just couldn't get in. The coppers were in the terrace that was empty and started to grab people through the railings. This bloke had the arm pulled off his coat as he pulled free and he was going mad. When the coppers finally did get in through the top, we all moved back. The Bolton lads were well out, but there was one of our lads there handcuffed to the railings. Poor fucker, he was shouting at us to get him out but there was nothing we could do. The coppers loved it and gave him a right hiding, which we could only watch. Then they arrested him. The Bolton lads were singing, 'Nice one copper, nice one son, nice one copper, go nick another one.' Well, you would.

The truth of the matter was that while the fences were good from a PR and containment viewpoint, they also had the effect of making some supporters play up even more, safe in the knowledge that they would never actually be able to get at the enemy! They also fostered resentment from the majority of perfectly innocent supporters, who took exception to being caged-in like animals. Abuse aimed at players and visiting fans increased, and on far too many terraces of the period the mood was of outright hatred.

A more dangerous consequence of the fences was the fact that those who saw physical confrontation as a routine, and often essential, part of their matchday began to take their activities out into the surrounding areas. This caused the police terrific problems, because while they could, to a certain extent, keep on top of things within the stadia, they had no concept of how to handle anything else. Once the fans saw this, trouble around grounds increased, and as the seventies wore on, supporters had begun to organise themselves into specific groups.

These groups could be as small as ten or fifteen people, but for the big clubs – Chelsea, West Ham, etc – a good day could see upwards of 1,500 turning out, and the 'safety in numbers' mentality displayed by these groups meant increased problems for the police. These groups quickly grew into almost secret cliques and within their membership there evolved a hierarchy of sorts: a leader, runners, scouts, etc, all with their own particular role within the group. As these groups evolved into the fighting firms or crews, some of them took nicknames to make it easier for opposing supporters to keep track of their exploits. Tales of Millwall's F-Troop and West Ham's ICF settled into legend.

Once these groups became organised and, more importantly, known, the police found it easier to keep track of them and their activities. The difficulty lay in finding out who the individual members were. It had long been suspected among travelling supporters that the police would rarely arrest anyone if they were part of a large firm, in case things kicked off, and this meant that they had no accurate records of offenders. Furthermore, the usual Metropolitan Police tactics for finding out who was who, such as checking accents and addresses, were totally ineffective at London derbies. They had to find a more reliable method of getting on top of the problem, and as far as they were concerned, the best way of doing this was to try to infiltrate the mobs with undercover officers.

In the early eighties, the Met adopted this as a key strategy against the hooligan groups and undertook large-scale operations against a number of London clubs, particularly Chelsea. The most famous of these was given the title of Operation 'Own Goal', a label that was to prove very apt. While details of the operation, for obvious reasons, remain somewhat sketchy, it is known that six undercover officers worked their way into a Chelsea firm (allegedly the Headhunters) and began gathering sufficient evidence to obtain convictions against the ringleaders. On 11 May 1986, following a trial that lasted in the region of 18 weeks and cost the taxpayer almost £3 million, five people were convicted of various offences including affray and conspiracy, and were jailed for a total of 28 years. Despite the fact that those convicted had almost 32 previous convictions between them, most of which were for violence, they quickly appealed and the Met, thinking it was on a sure thing, submitted some of the undercover officers' log-books for forensic analysis. Unfortunately for the police, this backfired as the forensic scientists cast doubt on the validity and accuracy of much of this evidence, claiming that some of the dates did not match and even that some had been falsified.

This was horrific news for the Met, who now suffered the humiliation of watching a number of undercover operations go down the pan, including those against Millwall, West Ham and Crystal Palace fans. Worse was to follow. On 17 October 1989, four alleged members of Millwall's notorious firm, the Bush-whackers, had their sentences cut on appeal, and on 17 November, three of the Chelsea supporters charged following 'Own Goal' had their convictions quashed on appeal. The following day, a fourth was released from prison after his original sentence was reduced from six to four years. In all, this made a total of 124 prosecutions arising from football hooliganism that had either collapsed or been altered on appeal. Despite this embarrassment, the police insisted that the tactic of undercover infiltration had not been abandoned.

From the outside and looking back, it is clear now that infiltration was a very risky method of trying to obtain a conviction, being totally reliant on the integrity of the officers concerned. Our own experiences and research have convinced us that it would be all but impossible to integrate yourself into a major firm without either breaking the law yourself or being party to a criminal act. For example, part of the evidence submitted from 'Own Goal' surrounded an incident at Goodison Park on 10 December 1985, when Chelsea supporters fought a pitched battle with Everton fans. The details of the incident, as told to the court, contained evidence that one of the undercover officers was party to both the planning and execution of the incident, which involved a Chelsea supporter being battered in the face with a wooden mallet and almost 40 supporters fighting in a sidestreet before uniformed officers arrived and broke up the brawl. The consequences of this incident were that people were trapped in their cars, property was damaged and locals, terrified for their own safety, were scattered in all directions. It is certainly arguable whether, in cases such as these, the ends really do justify the means. Judging by the small number of convictions that have arisen as a direct result of such operations, it is clear to us that they do not.

While Operation 'Own Goal' was still in progress, the Metropolitan Police were as good as handed a free rein to do whatever was needed to sort things out. This came about as a result of two major incidents involving London clubs, the riot at Stamford Bridge during the second leg of the Milk Cup semi-final against Sunderland and the Millwall riot at L*t*n. Both of these incidents are covered elsewhere, but the key thing about the riot at L*t*n was that at the time, the police believed that large numbers of hooligans from *other* clubs had gone up to Kenilworth Road with the express purpose of causing mayhem. They frequently quoted the swollen numbers of so-called 'Millwall fans' at the game as evidence, and with the Prime Minister being anti-football anyway, they did enough to convince Mrs Thatcher that legislation was needed urgently. This was hastened by events at Bradford (not hooligan-related, but another example of how shabby football had become) and Heysel, which dragged the reputation of football in this country even lower. Help from the government duly arrived in the shape of the Sporting Events Act 1985 (which dealt with alcohol), the Public Order Act 1986 (which allowed the banning of convicted offenders from grounds) and the Football Spectators Act 1989 (which allowed restriction-orders on travel and dealt with racist and abusive chanting). These measures gave the police some of the powers they had been seeking, and supporters began to realise that things would have to quieten down a bit. The police finally seemed to be gaining the upper hand, and another weapon became available to them which was to prove the single most valuable tool they had ever had at their disposal: closed-circuit television (CCTV).

CCTV had been around for a number of years. Indeed, it had been mooted as a good idea from the early seventies, but the improved technology and reduced cost meant that it was now becoming a more viable proposition. However, many clubs were still reluctant to install CCTV because of the cost, and once again the innocent fans were being put at risk. All that was finally to change after the tragedy at Hillsborough.

Lord Justice Taylor realised that CCTV was by far and away the most effective weapon against the hooligans. It would be absolutely essential if a return to the dark days of pitch-invasions was to be avoided when the fences came down, and Taylor understood that the fear of an early-morning visit from the police a few days after the match was enough to make even the most hardened of hooligans stop and think.

With the implementation of the 1991 Football Offences Act (which dealt with throwing objects, running on the pitch, etc), the tide had seemingly turned and hooligans were now under pressure from all sides. While the police supported all of these initiatives to the hilt, they also quickly realised that the dedicated firms, with years of rivalries and reputations behind them, would not simply vanish. The pubs, clubs and local streets would become the new battlegrounds. The Metropolitan Police also had another factor to consider, because for years many of the more dangerous battles had been fought in a different arena altogether, and one in which they had little real expertise: the London Underground.

Here, the Met at least had some help in the shape of the British Transport Police (BTP), who for years had been engaged in an ongoing struggle with the hooligans (who saw the tube network as the ideal place to carry on their war). Indeed, the BTP had instigated undercover operations of their own and were rumoured to have a network of informants inside many of the more well-known firms. The BTP are not known for their tolerance and, to put it bluntly, they do not piss about. In truth, they can't afford to, because the underground is a very dangerous place to be. The geography of London and the layout of a number of the stations mean that there is no room, or time, for error. In recent years, the increasing use of CCTV has again been a revelation to the underground officers, whose battle to defeat the hooligans has seen them achieve some amazing results.

By the early nineties, large-scale football hooliganism within the capital was on the decline. The running battles and pitch invasions within grounds had been all but confined to history, and the organised firms were now being tracked more easily via intelligence-gathering from both CCTV and co-ordinated police work (as technology improved, the Met's performance on the ground kept equal pace).

This success was a key factor in England being awarded Euro 96, and it was here that the police were to face their sternest test. A nationwide operation costing £10 million (or £20 million, depending on whose figures you believe) and involving thousands of policemen from all over the country was put in place to ensure that the tournament would pass off peacefully. The Metropolitan Police and the British Transport Police would of course be directly in the front line, because if anything was going to happen it would almost certainly be in London.

Prior to the tournament, the police went into PR overdrive to calm the fears of the general public (which had been largely whipped up by a hysterical media, desperate for a decent story). Through the National Criminal Intelligence Service (NCIS), they convinced everyone who would listen that they had all bases covered so nothing of any significance would happen. Television documentaries were glowing in their assessment of police planning and intelligence-gathering, and footage of senior officers visiting their colleagues in Germany or Holland became almost routine viewing. Furthermore, the police around the country went intelligence-crazy and just about every informant and known troublemaker was questioned or checked out. With the impact of Dublin still fresh in the minds of Mr and Mrs Average, many of the known political extremist groups were also targeted. The police mounted high-profile raids on known hooligans throughout England and arrested any number of people (most of whom, funnily enough, were released once the accompanying cameramen had gone home).

The Met were certainly at their busiest for some considerable time. A number of Spurs supporters were arrested after video footage of incidents in the North London derby at Highbury, and with Chelsea supporters, was analysed at length. Strangely, the Chelsea supporters who took part in the same incident were not produced, which led to claims that the Chelsea firm concerned contained undercover officers – the implication being that if footage of them were released, then they might be identified or even caught on film 'indulging' themselves, leading to yet another series of embarrassing court cases. The Met also adopted a number of new tactics during the tournament, including the use of the dreaded photographer and his 'photophone' (a brand new device that allowed photographs to be relayed directly to central headquarters, enabling the police to identify and keep track of possible offenders). Also the rather effective idea of spotting known troublemakers and following them around at very close quarters was adopted.

While the Met had a number of problems at pubs and clubs throughout the city during June 1996, the real problems took place in the West End and it was here, very nearly, that as far as the hooligans were concerned, they almost lost it completely.

Chapter 10
Altogether Now

During Euro 96, London was invaded by firms from all over the country. They came from Plymouth, Middlesbrough, Hull, everywhere, all hoping to get a piece of the action that the rest of Europe had promised. For the London mobs, the tournament posed even greater problems. Everyone was coming to their manor and because of that, each one had to put up a show, not only for our European visitors but for their fellow country-men as well. There was no way that they could let liberties be taken by anyone on their own patch, foreign or English. Add to that the simmering London club rivalries and you had potential mayhem.

A few days before the tournament was due to start, the police made a big show of arresting just six London fans in Operation 'Take Off'. This was meant to send shivers down the spine of every hooligan thinking of taking part in the anticipated violence on the capital's streets. Unfortunately for the police, a total of just six arrests, from an operation involving 70 officers and months of undercover work, made them a laughing stock. Mr and Mrs Average may have been impressed, but to those that mattered it was a farce.

The opening match was always going to go off quietly as Switzerland presented no problems. For the hooligan element, it offered up the chance to check the battleground and show their presence, while the pre-tournament hype and national expectation kept the rest of the country buzzing.

As mobs descended on the Globe pub opposite Baker Street tube, the police tactics became clear. They stopped, searched and questioned everybody that looked like a lad. The photographic squad were working overtime, providing Scotland Yard with what must be the ugliest photo-album ever known to man, and the surveillance team opposite filmed every move. The place was under siege, but that meant that the rest of London was going to be pretty much clear of police interruption.

As lads from all over the country came together under the banner of being English, there was one noticeable exception: the main London firms. They kept themselves apart, not only from the rest but also from the police and each other.

With Chelsea holed up in Ealing, and West Ham and Millwall staying on their own turf, the only real London presence came from the smaller clubs and a small group of Spurs. It was obvious that talk of some kind of 'Cockney Super Firm' was total bollocks that was never going to happen. London club loyalty would only be forgotten by those that shared a political belief. Otherwise, unlike the rest of the country, they would keep themselves to themselves and do their own thing.

As the Scotland game approached, tension and expectations mounted until finally a firm of Aberdeen kicked it off in Camden on the Thursday before the game. The Jocks had arrived and let everyone know they were more than up for it, it was game on. If the London mobs wanted a piece of the action, this time they would have to show.

Once again the mobs descended on the capital, only this time in even greater numbers. What had so far been an unexpectedly quiet tournament had started to swing into action. Stories of rows were spreading through the grapevine. What was surprising, though, was that rather than targeting the Scottish in Trafalgar Square, the English fans seemed to be settling a few old scores among themselves, such as Plymouth with Exeter and Portsmouth with Southampton. The police were starting to get stretched. Mobs were moving all over London via the tube network and buses, and some of the larger out-of-town firms, such as Leeds, didn't meet at the expected place, leaving large numbers of officers in the backstreets around King's Cross looking at empty pubs. London was buzzing.

Luckily, the atmosphere up at Wembley couldn't have been more different. Fans from both countries mingled without incident, which, considering the history that surrounds the fixture, came as a complete surprise to the police, the media and the majority of fans that attended. The hooligan element from both countries had decided that their fixture would take place well away from the national stadium, and as the police focused on the West End and Trafalgar Square, things were kicking off elsewhere.

The Scottish hard-core totalled around 200, mainly made up of Aberdeen, Dundee and Hibs, with Falkirk and Kilmarnock also putting in a show. In the same way that Arsenal and Spurs would never stand together, neither would the big two from north of the border, so both Rangers and Celtic were nowhere to be seen. Aberdeen Casuals had been running the show as far as the Scots were concerned, kicking it off before the match with Millwall in Tottenham Court Road, Middlesbrough in Leicester Square and Chelsea at Cambridge Circus. What was clear was that the Scots, after initial problems between Aberdeen and Dundee fans, were prepared to fight alongside each other, unlike the English at this stage. It was also clear that none of these groups were intending to make it to the match.

Once the final whistle went, Trafalgar Square became the focal point, with the Scottish hard-core paying their first visit to Nelson's Column. As the Scottish numbers grew, the violence from the English fans became more sporadic. While Birmingham, Oxford and Colchester were teaming-up to have a pop at the Sweaties, the other main mobs were congregating at the Porcupine pub by Leicester Square tube. The police were caught in the middle as small groups of English fans used every sidestreet they could to get at the Scots, who were already engaged in running battles with the riot squad. The police were once again near to breaking-point when a relatively small incident took place at the

Porcupine. Frustration at attempts to bring things together among the English fans sparked off violence involving small mobs of Chelsea and Spurs after some Chelsea fans, on their return from a raid on the Square, had taunted their rivals. The police, thinking this was it, deployed every officer they could muster into the area. Van after van-load of police pulled up, unloading its cargo of baton-happy bobbies, leaving the route down into Trafalgar Square wide open.

As groups of Leicester and Sunderland fans tried in vain to get everyone together, most of the other mobs seemed to be more interested in a possible confrontation with the police. It was at this point that the police made a vital breakthrough, as the decision was made to force the Scottish support down into the tube and get them away before the English mobs woke up to the situation. Whoever made that decision saved the day as far as the police were concerned. The full meeting of the two hooligan groups had been avoided.

Having been involved in running battles with fans from both sides for most of the night, the police finally had some sort of control over the situation. Once the English fans had 'reclaimed' Trafalgar Square, the police were in no mood to let the party drag on for too long and soon moved in to break it up. They had made over 80 arrests, and used CS gas and baton-charges in order to keep things under control. Mounted officers and dog handlers had been deployed, and numerous people had ended up needing hospital treatment, yet the commander in charge described the whole incident as 'a little over-exuberance'. In truth, it could have been much worse.

As the police wiped their brows, most of the mobs from around the country pointed the finger at the London firms for missing the opportunity to pay the Scots back once and for all for their invasion of Wembley in 1977. It could even be said that the Scots had once again put on a better show and come out on top.

The next match was against Holland and again the police were on full alert. But for those intent on violence, this fixture was a non-starter as it was clear that the Dutch had once again bottled out. With the game being in midweek, the hooligan presence in

London was kept down to a minimum. The team's display, the subsequent result and the elimination of the Scottish, thanks to the late Dutch goal, kept London quiet.

The quarter-final tie against Spain prompted violence of a different kind. The Spanish national side, like the Dutch, had no hooligan following despite the violence in their own domestic league. But the match, played on a Saturday afternoon, allowed the whole of the country to indulge in an all-day drinking festival. The fact that England won the fixture did little to stop outbreaks of violence throughout the country. In Enfield, a suburb of North London, a double-decker bus was nearly rocked onto its side as passengers fled for their safety, while a traffic warden was beaten up and had his moped set on fire. The capital was on red alert for the next match, a semi-final against the Germans.

Like the English, the German national side was known to have a travelling hooligan element intent on causing trouble. In the months prior to the tournament, they had issued 'warnings' to the English by rioting in both Belgium and Holland, and for them London would prove the ultimate test.

Despite the match being played in midweek, the capital was swarming with mobs from all over the country desperately looking for the German mob, but as the day passed it became clear that, like the Dutch, the Germans didn't have the stomach for it. The reputation they had built up throughout Europe was shot down in one day, and for the English, who were pumped up to defend their reputation, this boiled over into frustration and, ultimately, violence. After the match, trouble started to flare up between rival English mobs when Millwall fans attacked a group of Norwich supporters in Bond Street, as it became clear that some of the London firms had had enough of the rest of the country coming to their home ground and taking liberties. Elsewhere in the country, following Gareth Southgate's penalty-miss there was violent disorder, but nowhere was to witness scenes like those in central London. Nearly every mob in the capital made their way to Trafalgar Square and, with no foreigners to target, we finally saw the coming together of all the English mobs to do battle with the old enemy, the police.

Throughout the tournament, the police had pushed their luck and done themselves no favours at all in the public-relations stakes. Many people had been stopped over and over again, searched and photographed, and their anger had reached boiling-point. For the mobs, Trafalgar Square offered an opportunity for a little payback, an opportunity that wasn't going to be missed.

The crowd lashed out at anything that moved as the police struggled to restore some kind of order. With their officers simply outnumbered, the police just took to sending in the riot squad on one side while another section of the mob smashed up cars, buses and people on the other. Once the numbers started to reduce, the real battle between the police and the hard-core got underway. As the two sides charged and taunted each other, one in full riot-gear, the other armed with bottles and cans, Japanese and American tourists filmed every move: football violence for the beginner. As the night wore on, the mobs dispersed leaving London to clear up the mess, as pictures were shown throughout the world that maybe justified the decision to stay at home by the Dutch and Germans.

Once England were knocked out, the tournament appeared to be over as far as the country was concerned. The capital breathed a sigh of relief as the Germans even failed to show for the final. As the police, the FA and UEFA all patted themselves on the back in public, the scene behind closed doors must have been very different. They all knew that the hooligan element were also rubbing their hands, after sending another message out to the world that the home of football violence was still ready to take on all-comers.

As the FA continues to try and kid the average armchair fan and potential sponsors that football violence is a thing of the past, it is worth noting one final thing. During Euro 96, mobs from all over the country came to the capital and let their presence be known. This show opened up many old rivalries, as well as starting up a few new ones. For the London firms, there is something to prove after allowing so many mobs to come and run freely around the streets of central London. As far as many are concerned, the failure of the so-called 'police intelligence' has reopened the whole game, a game that the hooligans feel they won during June 1996.

Equally, there is no doubt that the Metropolitan Police will have learnt a lot during Euro 96 and that the policing of football in the capital should improve as a result. They put on a good show for the tourists and the cameras, but for those of us who spent time in the West End during the tournament, and were treated appallingly for no reason other than the fact that we were there, it was an outrage. Before and after the Scotland match, the police had no choice but to act, and it must be said that they played a major role in containing the violence at the level it was. If only they had left well alone and kept a discreet distance following the Germany game, things might have turned out better than they could possibly have prayed for. Instead, by trying to make a point (and no doubt justify the cost), they provoked a mass violent reaction with their deployment of hordes of riot gear-clad policemen in the Square. They must acknowledge that in this instance they got it wrong, big time.

We are already on record as saying that we are no fans of the police because of the way they treat supporters, and that opinion has not changed one iota. However, we recognise that they have a difficult and at times dangerous job to do, and that if people did not fight at football then there would be no need for the police to be there at all. We, as fans and former hooligans, may be critical of their performance – but for some, isn't it simply a case of their getting the police force they deserve?

If the police have a hard enough time keeping on top of it all in the domestic game, then the travelling England fans pose another set of problems altogether. Whenever England play abroad, it is clear that most football firms are happy to leave their domestic rivalries behind. Of course, local rivals can never be trusted – obviously Manchester City and United fans would never fight side by side, nor would fans of Newcastle and Sunderland – but there are firms with fierce, distant rivalries that are prepared to come together under the national flag. The following account comes from Birmingham City fan, J.

MILLWALL, BRUM, ROTTERDAM

We were making our way over to Rotterdam for the World Cup qualifier in '93. The ferry is always interesting, it's the first chance to get an idea of just who is making the journey and gives some clue to the kind of firm you're going to get.

There were about 200 lads on the ferry, so turning up in Holland was going to be pretty safe and looked like fun. There were a group of about 30 Leeds lads that were playing up, trying to take centre stage. They were giving loads of verbal to these Forest fans, really taunting them. Loads of other lads were looking on, and just as it looked like getting nasty, one of our lads started to have a go at the Leeds boys. We were worried that if things kicked off here, then they would turn the ferry back and all of us would miss out just because of a few mouthy Yorkshire twats. Our lad figured that if we backed up the Forest lads then we would have the numbers to sort the Leeds firm out if it got out of hand. The Leeds soon shut it – they couldn't have been top lads, because Leeds don't do that. The Forest lads also didn't want any of it.

We were stood waiting for some kind of response when these other lads walked over, a couple of them wearing Millwall shirts. Now us and Millwall don't get on and at first I thought this was going to go, but they asked if we wanted to have a beer instead. They turned out to be top lads and they were going to Rotterdam for one thing, to have it with the Dutch. We decided to stick together making a nice little firm of around 25 Zulus and Millwall, tops. Once we got to Ostend, we got away from the rest of the English lads and made our own way into Holland. We talked a bit about our own rivalry but not too much, we were all English lads together from the top two cities doing it for the country. It's funny because if we came across each other when England were at Wembley, we would probably have it away; that's the game, I suppose.

The Millwall lads had a good idea of where the local

Feyenoord firm drank, so we settled in a pub nearby. After a while, these Scousers came in and told us that they had just scouted the Feyenoord bar and the locals were forming up and getting a bit loud. It was time to move in. As we got to the corner, it became clear that the Dutch had been tipped off that we were on our way. They were all out in the street, about 150 I reckoned. They started throwing bottles and glasses and moving forward, but this firm of Brummies and Cockneys were going nowhere. We grabbed the chairs from the cafes and steamed into them. Once they seen us coming, they turned on their toes and shot off down the side-roads. We got up to the corner by the bar when, from the sidestreet, they started firing flares at us. We were bombing along, fighting for England and we didn't give a fuck, we were at them again. These wankers were great at throwing things and running but shit at fighting. These were meant to be Holland's number-one firm, cloggy wankers. I don't know what it was, whether we were trying to outdo each other or what, but we were all going mental. I think it was mostly that we all knew we could trust the other firm's lads, and that's the kind of back-up you need on foreign soil.

The police came flying down the road and blocked us off, then pushed us back towards their bar. Once the police arrived, the Dutch lads suddenly became very brave and steamed down as well, knowing they couldn't get near us. At this point, a group of around 300 lads turned the corner from where we had originally come. It was the main English firm. I would love to know what went through the Dutch fans' minds, I've never seen a mob disappear so fast. The police couldn't handle us at all, as there were only about 40 of them there then. As the Dutch did the off, we turned on the bar and all the windows went through.

None of us had tickets for the match, so we joined the main firm and spent the day charging around the streets of Rotterdam before making our way to the stadium. Here we decided to split from the Millwall lads, as it might make it easier to get in. As it was, we had to go back to the bar and watch the game on TV. We saw the Cockneys the next night in Amsterdam, chilling out. They had missed the game as well. They had hung around the ground and headed straight back to the station after the game, where things had really kicked off. They said the local lads were nowhere, so they had gone straight to Amsterdam with around 200 others to see if Ajax had any lads out looking for it, but had got no joy.

That was a great trip. We've had it with Millwall many times and I've got great respect for their firm. These lads were top boys, a good laugh and great to stand and fight with. Trouble is, next season back home we won't be fighting *with* them.

As Europe becomes an ever smaller place, the opportunities for the hooligans to take their activities further afield increase. The police forces of Europe are now working together to combat another, less publicised, problem.

Chapter 11
European Links

While the British government and the police were busy keeping the violence that surrounded Euro 96 off our screens, the media throughout Europe were happily beaming the English football hooligans' activities into every living-room on the continent. As the English fought with the Scottish, the police and each other, our European cousins were keen to make play of the fact that the English football thug wasn't a thing of the past.

Throughout Europe, football violence is rife with almost every country suffering from the 'English Disease'. What the pictures from Euro 96 achieved was to place the English firmly back at the top of the table and return them to God-like status in the minds of the European hooligans. The latter continue to look to England for their lead and are known to try hard to form links with the top firms in this country. Anyone watching European football on satellite TV cannot fail to notice the number of Union Jacks on display at matches, often bearing English team names, particularly in Germany and Holland. Some of this can be put down to the fact that there are many football-starved servicemen based there, but not all the links are as innocent as they may first appear.

Once again it is the London clubs that are at the forefront of hooligan-related links with the Europeans. In the same way that the English football casual wears top gear to identify himself,

Chelsea, West Ham and Millwall scarves are often worn in Germany by their hooligans. No style, these foreigners! Often scarves will be made up half in the colours of the local club, with the other half coming from the adopted English side.

Chelsea hooligans with connections to the far-right have become linked to many European clubs' supporters due to sharing the same political beliefs, and this is evident in Sweden, Germany, France and Italy. In Germany the hooligan fanzine *Fan Treff* often prints detailed accounts of fighting between rival English firms, particularly those from London. These accounts focus on tactics, police manoeuvres and arrest-figures, as well as giving a league table of the top firms in England and Germany. When the magazine first started, the readership struggled to reach the 500-mark; but after printing an account of a West Ham–Millwall battle, they found that sales shot up to 3,000! Another article in the fanzine, a feature on the Chelsea Headhunters, led to the use of the 'calling card' by German and Dutch firms. It is within Holland that the links with English clubs appear to be strongest. Ajax, known for their violent following, have strong links with the Spurs hooligans, resulting from Tottenham's violent clashes with Ajax's main rivals, Feyenoord of Rotterdam, and also from the strong Jewish links both clubs hold. Last season, when Feyenoord played Ajax in Amsterdam, a joint Ajax/Tottenham firm fought running battles with the Rotterdam club's supporters, whose numbers were swollen in turn by visiting Chelsea fans. The street battles continued throughout the night as the London clubs' firms took their hatred for each other one step further.

The European firms will often visit their London counterparts to 'learn the trade', as one group put it. In the early nineties, Feyenoord supporters had been busy building links with the Millwall firm and had been invited to London to take part in some post-match activity. Supporters of Ajax also had loose connections there and were tipped off about this visit, resulting in their arrival in London at the same time as their Dutch rivals. As battle commenced, the Feyenoord fans were soon on their toes as their bottle went, losing any respect the Millwall fans had for them. On seeing this, the Ajax firm went in hot pursuit of their countrymen, taking them by complete surprise, and gave them a run as well. The incident ended up forging greater links between Ajax and Millwall, as the Londoners could only admire the show put up by the lads from Amsterdam in order to put one over their main rivals. Millwall fans were also known to have been present in the Amsterdam confrontation mentioned above.

Ajax are also said to have links with Arsenal and West Ham as well as clubs from outside the capital such as Newcastle, Liverpool, Man City, Forest, Leeds and Burnley. These links may partly explain why the Dutch national side never carries the same violent following when the two countries meet as their league clubs do when English and Dutch teams play each other. The Dutch league consists of very few firms who could or would hold their own against the top English mobs. Whenever England play, most club rivalries are set aside and sheer weight of numbers is enough to deter all but the most determined opposition, such as the Scots.

Another group that tried to forge links with Millwall were fans of the Belgian side FC Bruges – but not all such attempts are successful.

UNWELCOME VISITORS

We had visited Millwall on a few trips. To us they were the most famous and frightening football hooligans in England, with great respect. We travelled to see them play at Aston Villa in 1988, their first away game in Division One, as we thought they would take a lot of hooligans to this match. We decided to try and make contact with their ringleaders on the train but, after trying, it was clear that they didn't want to talk to us. There were five of us, and as the train travelled the Millwall fans started to call us 'foreign bastards' and were telling us to 'fuck off back home'. It became very scary as there were so many of them, and they were all old men and very aggressive to us.

When the train arrived, there were hundreds of Millwall so we waited until they had all gone. There were lots of policemen as well as other supporters from other teams. It was not like in Belgium and was a hard atmosphere. We went to the game in the Villa part of the ground. These fans were also very aggressive and the atmosphere was fantastic. FC Bruges like Chelsea fans most, and I was pleased they beat the Millwall fans. We go to Stamford Bridge at least four times a season.

Chapter 12
Have The Hooligans Got It 'Sorted'?

As the government, the football authorities and the police went on the offensive in their quest to combat the football hooligan, help was at hand from a very unexpected and unlikely source. Along came another movement that, for many, was able to replace the buzz that football violence gave them. From the mid-eighties, the dance and rave culture that swept the country offered an alternative high that many found irresistible, and its effect on the hooligans should not be underestimated.

The football hooligan was having to face up to the fact that the police, for the first time, were finally coming out on top. The high that he craved had been taken away and needed to be replaced with something, so dance music, and the drugs that went with that scene, couldn't have come along at a better time (both for the police and the hooligan).

The drugs acid and ecstasy, unlike alcohol, are not fighting drugs; quite the opposite. Ecstasy, known as the love drug, gives users a feeling of elation and love for all that is around them. Fighting would be the last thing to enter the mind, and indeed the opportunity to go out and enjoy the rush without the threat of having your head battered certainly had its bonuses. Those who indulged in football violence on a regular basis often knew the names and faces of the opposition, and with the growth in the rave movement, they often found themselves at the same clubs and all-nighters as their fiercest rivals. Whereas in a drinking atmosphere this would undoubtedly have resulted in violence, the nature of the drug scene saw an openness and coming together of many rival groups, as old rivalries were set aside. After all, these people had come from the same movement and had an awful lot in common. Both in London and the rest of the country, the police were surprised to find firms from Chelsea and Spurs, or Leeds and Man United, openly mixing together without the threat of trouble. For the police, this was a major result.

Many of the larger firms found another use for this movement, the opportunity to make money by organising the raves and dealing in drugs. This simply gave the police an added weapon in their fight against the hooligans, as they now had additional information on the individuals and ringleaders which they used to great effect. The use of drugs is illegal, and when an officer turns up at a match and starts asking if you will be out popping pills later that night, then you know that they have you by the balls and it is time to get out.

The dance movement continues to grow stronger and stronger, but for those who were there at the beginning, the novelty has started to wear off. Many see all-nighters as a young man's game, and the thrill of the pills is slowly being replaced by a return to the beer culture and to football. We believe that the re-emergence of football violence is connected to the return of some of the older faces, who are now seeking out the buzz they used to enjoy so much.

PART SIX
North London

Chapter 13
Arsenal – Home Of The Invisible Mob?

When we research our books, we do it in a simple yet usually efficient manner. We contact everybody we know, and write to everybody who has ever written to us and ask for their opinions and anecdotes. If Watford aren't playing, we go to games and visit pubs and clubs and talk to people face-to-face, write letters to fanzines, and spend countless hours in reference libraries and newspaper archives to filter through all the crap and get, as near as we possibly can, to the truth. Lately, we have even taken to spending time on the club-talk pages on the Internet, but they are inhabited by such sad bastards we have abandoned that avenue, at least for now.

For some clubs, this method of research is easier than others. West Ham and the ICF are a good example of that. After all, they've been up to enough trouble over the years to make finding out about them easy for anyone who cares to look. But Arsenal have been a different case entirely. No matter how much we've asked around at other clubs or how many times we've been down to Highbury on matchdays (and thanks to the demands of television that's a few) no one can, or will, tell us anything of any real value. Everyone knows the club have, particularly in the early to mid-eighties, had an active mob. Many supporters, including the two of us, have been on the receiving end of their attentions on more than one occasion. The trouble is that almost everything we hear is the same: no spectacular incidents, no massive pre-planned offs, nothing.

The club should be proud of that fact, as should the vast majority of the Arsenal support who, like us, are totally against hooliganism and want rid of it for good. But, for the purposes of this book, written as it has been to expose the background to the London hooliganism scene, Arsenal are just not interesting enough. They have proved to be the Steve Davis of football firms!

We do know, for example, that Arsenal fans have been abroad with England in the past and have been to Europe with their club and caused trouble on numerous occasions, just as we know that individual Arsenal fans were targeted during the infamous Operation 'Own Goal', and also that a number were arrested during the build-up to Euro 96. But we know only part of the story and if people don't give us the facts, we can't put it down within these pages. For example, during the 1996–97 season, rumours were rife that a number of small hooligan groups were indulging in a feud to establish who was the top firm at Highbury. We were told that by three different people, but other normally reliable sources shook their heads in bewilderment when we asked them about it, so who should we have believed? We have even heard rumours that there is a serious racism problem among the fans at Highbury. This came as something of a surprise to us considering the colour of some of Arsenal's best players, and many of their supporters. There have been rumours that Ian Wright dislikes going near a certain area of Highbury, even after he has scored. But, again, they have been impossible to confirm or disprove. We know full well that we will be bombarded with letters from angry Gunners giving us grief, but all we can do is apologise in advance. If nothing else, it shows that although we could have written any old bollocks, and no one but the Gooners themselves would have been any the wiser, that would have served no purpose at all.

During the early eighties, the Arsenal firm were undoubtedly at their most active and had one of the most volatile firms in the capital, the main bulk of it made up of various mobs from the New Towns in Hertfordshire and the west of Essex. Once Watford arrived in the top flight, this pitched us against the Arsenal and brought us into confrontation with these mobs, some of whom came from the same town as ourselves. This extra twist to the rivalry seemed to spur the Gooners on even more, and although they didn't have such large numbers as some of the other London clubs, the Arsenal boys probably went for Watford more than any other.

UP THE ARSE . . . NAL

We couldn't wait to have a go at Watford. All I got at work was Watford this, Watford that, as they were on the way up. I knew a few lads that liked an off and they went on and on about how they ran Brentford, did this and that, as if I really fucking cared. We used to wind each other up no end about what would happen if we ever met and then bingo, we were drawn to play them at their place in an FA Cup quarter-final.

There was loads going on in the build-up to this match, every Gooner I knew was up for this and the talk at the home games was of nothing else. The Watford lads were still giving it some; at one point even I was starting to get a bit worried. I mean, getting turned over by Watford was something I would never be able to live with.

On the day of the match we made our own way in, as did all the other firms. We were all out for doing our own thing as we knew who we were looking for and the police wouldn't be able to hold onto every mob if we were spread out. All the Arsenal lads were out, we took the town over and the Watford boys were nowhere to be seen before the game. Every pub in the town centre was Arsenal.

As there was no action before the game, we were going to try the home end and see if we could get in. It was like the queue for the Clock End, nearly all Arsenal, but the stewards were pointing people out to the Old Bill and most of the Gooners were directed down to our end after pleading innocence as to what end they were up. We made it in, and as we got through the turnstile we saw some of the Watford lads. They clocked us straight away, which sent the old arsehole going a bit, and a few of the lads went for it there and then, dishing out a few slaps before getting dragged out by the coppers. We slipped along the side and waited in the corner.

We could see the coppers moving in over at the turnstiles on the opposite side, which must have been the same sort of thing kicking off. We didn't have a clue how many Gooners were in here and there were plenty of their lot buzzing around not knowing who was who either, but slowly we were joined by some of the other lads and this was turning into a tidy little firm.

The problem with mobbing-up in an away end is that you soon start to stand out from those around you, and as we were surrounded by old boys, it wasn't long before we noticed a few of their lot slowly turning up waiting for it to happen. So we went for it. That's a great moment, seeing all those around you move off, leaving you waiting for their mob to have a go. Their boys around us stood off, giving it loads of mouth and that, but we could see loads more of them running over from under the scoreboard. That was the time to steam in, it's no good waiting for them to get their numbers up, so in we went.

That was a great row, the Old Bill took ages to get there so we had it going for a fair while. We would steam in, then they would have a go back as we stood the ground we had taken. It was great in those days, steaming on the terraces. Once they got themselves sorted we were well outnumbered and, just when we needed them, the Old Bill turned up and got in between us. I started to see a few faces in their mob, which made it even better. They would have to live with this and I have rammed it down their throats ever since. All the Gooners down the other end were singing to us, and the police kept us where we were for most of the match, so we could take the piss even more. It kept going off as they would steam in every now and then and the coppers would move in on them to drag their lads out. They were going mental because the Old Bill were only nicking them, it was a great atmosphere. The police finally moved us around to these gates, then took us out and down our own end to join the lads and enjoy the praise.

After the match, the Arsenal mob was massive. The Old Bill seemed to double in number and were all over us. There had been at least one stabbing before the game and the coppers were in no mood to fuck about, but they couldn't keep us together and we easily gave them the slip. I was sure that Watford would get mobbed-up after what had happened, so we really wanted to get back into the town centre. The place was crawling with little mobs but there were so many coppers that nothing happened. So we went home to look for our local Watford lads and have it away with them.

West Ham, Chelsea and Millwall all had a go at the Watford end when they came to Vicarage Road, but Arsenal also went for the kill when we first visited Highbury in November 1982. A Watford fan recalls:

A HORNETS NEST

We had just dicked Spurs at White Hart Lane and were taking the First Division by storm. The away support was fantastic at that time and as the numbers grew, so did the hooligan element that followed the club. Going to places like Highbury and fronting it out was what it was all about, but trips to the big games in London in those days were always tinged with apprehension, as the London clubs had taken a massive dislike to the long-ball team that was taking the piss whenever we played them.

We travelled down on the train, not mob-handed, just the six of us getting off at Highbury and Islington tube and walking up that way. There were a few little groups of Arsenal hanging around but nothing to get worried about.

We knew they were going to have a go as the local Gooners had been giving it the big 'un, but all the way to the ground it was quiet. There were plenty of Watford about and the odd group of lads were hanging around; like us, they hadn't seen anything so in we went with some relief.

Once we got in the ground, it was a different story. The Clock End was rammed and was supposed to be half Watford, half Arsenal, but we were soon told that there were plenty of Gooners in with us and it was all boiling-up to go off any minute. The police didn't have a clue who was who, and the same went for most of the fans up that end as well. Everyone was trying to suss out what the fuck was going on. We were told that Watford had mobbed-up at the top of the stand and that the numbers were good with plenty of the old boys turning out, as they often did for the big games in those days.

We got up to the top and it was buzzing, every new Hornet being welcomed in as the numbers got bigger. Then came the charge from the Arsenal lads. They came in from both sides with everything flying. As we tried to fight back, we were forced down the terrace and they got up behind us, giving them the best position to steam in again. I remember looking around at my mate and saying to him that they were everywhere. The bloke behind him said, 'Yeah, I know, we're fucking everywhere. Come on, you cunt.' I shit myself, he was fucking massive. My mate got a punch in the back of the head followed by a boot up the arse. I saw one of the Watford lads having a go at a copper as more Gooners climbed the fence and came through the gates. He got hit with a truncheon and the copper tried to get the cuffs on. A couple of lads steamed in on the copper and he went down, that's when we started to fight back. He got a right hiding as he was trapped up against the fence, unable to get away. It served the cunt right, it's always nice to get one back on the Met. Our boy was pulled clear and off he went to keep his head down.

We slowly got our numbers back together and the police

finally arrived and got in between us and them. The Arsenal numbers had shrunk as most of their lads had done what they set out to do, give us a right hiding. As the game went on, it kept going off as some of the Arsenal had moved off in smaller mobs but stayed in with us. There were a few victories along the way: at half-time, a couple of Arsenal lads were given a right pasting down by the toilets. I saw them getting carried out the exit by the police and St John's, and they were in a right mess. The Hornets went on to take the piss, winning 4–2, and every goal kicked something off. But as the game went on, their numbers got less and less.

The final whistle went and the thought of getting back on the tube had me and the lads shitting ourselves. It's the same old story: if all the Watford lads would have stuck together, we would have a tidy mob – but as always, everyone goes their own way and tries to keep their heads down. The police let us out straight away, which was the last thing I wanted, but out we went expecting the Arsenal to steam us at any second. It didn't happen, they had done the off. What a result.

We made our way back down to Highbury tube and as we went, we could spot a fair few fellow Hornet lads doing the same thing as us and keeping their heads down. Then as this group of about five lads passed this bus stop, this small group of Arsenal started to give them some verbal. The Watford lads stopped, then one of the Gooners came forward and whacked one bloke in the face and a row breaks out. My mate that had been hit in the ground was in straight-away, after a bit of revenge, so in we went after him. There must have been about twenty Watford lads come out of nowhere, but my mate was the only one of us to get hit back as the Arsenal lads did the off. He was having one of those days! Unfortunately, when something like that happens you blow your cover and it was still a long way back to the tube station. The whole lot of us decided to watch each other's backs and move off down to the Angel tube, just in case these Arsenal lads went and got mobbed-up and came back looking for us. Luckily, they didn't. We split from the rest and went down to the West End for a few beers, meeting up with some other Watford fans. They said the tube was well naughty as the Arsenal fans were going mental after the result, hitting anyone wearing yellow, black and red.

Looking back, it was a great day out, everything you could want from going to football. We took the piss on the park, had a massive row in the ground which, although they did the business, ended up with only one of our lot getting a slap, and had a bit of a result ourselves on the way home. But no other London club has ever gone after us like Arsenal did that season.

The North London rivalry is as passionate as any in the country. For the hooligans, any meeting with their local rivals is likely to provoke violence, yet sometimes they turn up when least expected. Stuart tells of an unusual meeting.

WOMBLING THE SCUM

Being an Arsenal fan, there is nothing I hate more than our neighbouring scum, Tottering Blotspurs. I fucking hate them, their team, their ground, manager, their drab colours, that sad fucking pigeon they use for the club crest, but most of all I hate their sad bastard pathetic fans.

Me and me mates had been to watch the Gooners play Wimbledon at Highbury. If you have ever been to one of these matches, then you will know what a sad example of the English game they are. The FA should do away with the fixture and just give each club a point and save us all the money and the misery. After the usual sad game, we headed off down to the Essex Road to have a few bevvies as normal, a post-match ritual. As we reached the traffic lights at the bottom of Highbury Grove, we came across these Wimbledon lads who really gave us the big 'un. Well, I suppose even Wimbledon must have a few lads. There were seven or eight of them and four of us, not too bad odds so we went for it. As soon as we made a move they were off, through the backstreet onto Canonbury Road and down towards Essex Road station. We would usually have let the wankers go, but as they were heading towards our local we continued after them. Whenever we stopped running, so did they. We finally gave it one last burst as we neared the pub, then the Wimbledon lads ran up to a group of lads at a bus stop and waited. We thought they were mobbing-up and the numbers were starting to get a bit out of our favour. Then, out of the blue, they started rowing with these other lads. We're stood there wondering what the fuck was going on, when one of the Wimbledon lads comes towards us and shouts that this other lot were Yids.

We don't need a second offer where the scum are concerned, so we steamed in as well. They were on their heels straightaway, but we caught two of them and they took an almighty hiding. One of them wasn't moving and the other was pleading for us to stop, saying they had had enough. But you can never give too much to the scum, and these same wankers would do exactly the same to us, the Wimbledon lads, or whoever if the boot was on the other foot. That's the way it goes. I don't suppose the Wimbledon lads get that much action and they wanted to make the most of it. It turned out they had been run by the Yids before we saw them, so they had goaded us back down to give the Yids a kicking as a bit of payback, and they loved it. They turned out to be good lads, considering they came from south of the river, and I could only admire their nerve. We even offered to take them for a beer but they fucked off instead.

Another story that made us laugh was the one told to us by G. B. We both know how he feels.

TRAGIC MALE HAIR LOSS

I was brought up in Potters Bar, Hertfordshire, a real shithole of a place with nothing to do but hang around in little gangs scaring old ladies and bullying little kids. I've never been an aggressive bloke and got into music very early on, particularly rockabilly and all that went with it. As with any school, there were the usual bullies and being the only fifteen-year-old for miles around with a quiff, I came in for my fair share of stick and tried to keep as far away from 'the lads' as possible. The day I left that place was the greatest day of my life. Nearly all the kids in the school followed Arsenal, probably because it's only a few stops down on the train, and I was no different. I loved football and was always in the school first-team, which as far as the lads were concerned was my only saving grace.

After leaving school, I soon got a job and could afford to go to Highbury more often; me, my sister and her boyfriend, standing up the North Bank shouting our heads off. As we made our way back to Finsbury Park station after one home game, I could see all my ex-schoolmates. They were your typical football-thug casual types, real tossers walking around like they owned the place. The last thing I wanted was to bump into those idiots, so I asked my sister if we could wait a while, get a bag of chips and catch the next train up.

After about half an hour we went up onto the platform and, thank God, there was no sign of them. Just as the train was due, all the lads from school suddenly came running up the stairs, all shouting and mucking about. They spotted me straightaway, came over and at first started asking how I was doing and being all right really. They seemed pretty pissed and had a load of older lads with them who were probably their brothers or something. After we got on the train, these older lads started to have a go at the way I was dressed and the others all joined in, patting my hair down and ruffling it up, which really started to get on my nerves.

Then one of the lads flicked his ash in my hair and stubbed his fag out on my jacket, and for some unknown reason I lashed out and caught him straight in the mouth. For a second the whole world seemed to go quiet as they all stared at me, and my sister and her bloke melted into their seats and into open space. I was all alone.

The words 'Hit him back, Dave' broke the silence, but Dave didn't move. In the five years I had spent with these lads, they had never known me to raise my voice, let alone my fists, and they were stunned into silence. Maybe, just maybe, this rockabilly was a nutter, the silent type that comes and waits for you in your garden in the middle of the night then kneecaps you without warning, or cuts the brake-pipes on your car, killing you in a horrible head-on accident and leaving no clue as to who did it.

'Sorry, Dave.' The words sounded pathetic as Dave stood there with water in his eyes and blood on his lips. If I had meant it, it would have been a good thump.

'Fuck sorry, you nonce.' Bodies jumped on me from all sides, knocking me back onto the seat as they tried and tried to pummel my head in. 'Right, hold him down.' One of the older lads had taken charge and they pinned me on the floor, two on each arm and leg and the main one sitting on my chest with his knees forcing down my shoulders. 'Right, Dave, do the honours, mate.' From out of his pocket he pulled a Swiss-army knife and opened out the scissors. 'Cut that fucking stupid hair off.'

No, surely they didn't mean it, not my quiff. Fear welled up inside, along with the tears, and I screamed the place down. They were roaring with laughter and cheering themselves on. Dave couldn't bring himself to do it, but there were plenty willing to take their turn and once the first few chunks were taken off, resistance was pointless. As these tits ran around using my hair as makeshift quiffs for themselves, my sister cried her eyes out and her boyfriend didn't know whether to laugh with the lads or support his girl and risk a slap himself, the poor sod. Mum was horrified when I got home and wanted to ring the local paper to let the world know what these 'hoodlums' had done to her eighteen-year-old little soldier. I don't think I really needed that at the time.

In a town like Potters Bar, a story like that gets around pretty quick. I had to listen to it retold time and time again, with a brave smile on my face as if to say 'Ah, weren't they the good old days', when the truth was that that incident ruined my social life for about six months and has probably left me mentally scarred for life, deep down in my subconscious mind. Even my sister, who at the time was in a state of real distress, recalls the moment with great joy, the bitch. I no longer live up that way, thank God, leaving that shithole to fester in its own pool of pus. Yes, they were unhappy times.

I never have to use Finsbury Park station now or go in the North Bank, choosing to place myself elsewhere in the ground away from the morons.

Since that day, I've been a big believer in karma and just a year or so after that incident, I saw some of these braindeads at an away match. To my immense delight, I noticed that two of them had started to recede in the old hair department, and there was I with a fully regrown quiff. What goes around comes around.

Chapter 14
Come On You Spurs

If things had been only slightly different, it is highly likely that the two of us would have been spared the frustration, anger and disappointment that seems to be an integral part of supporting Watford. This is because Spurs are our old man's team and while it is fair to say that he is hardly the most active supporter we've ever met, he was a regular down the Lane in his youth and used to bore us senseless with tales of Blanchflower and Mackay. This in itself should have been enough of a lead for most sons, and even though he had moved out of London in the fifties, we should, by rights, have followed in his footsteps, just as we expect our sons to follow in ours.

However, if this was his intention, he made one fatal mistake that all but ensured our defection. Quite simply, his error was not taking us to White Hart Lane to see our first-ever live game. Instead, he took us to Vicarage Road for a crap 0–0 draw against Bristol Rovers. At that point, the seeds were sown and we have suffered for it ever since. After all, surely our supporting lives would have been more exciting if we had followed the North London giants around top division England, rather than traipsing after the Hornets in the lower depths? (Actually, we take that back!) Much as we love our club, it is a question we ponder all too frequently. Tottenham are a massive club and were undoubtedly once one of the biggest names in European football.

179

They have a long and distinguished history as a competitive club, yet that history is also littered with incidents of hooliganism, including some of the earliest recorded examples.

In 1880, two groups of schoolboys from different North London schools got together to form The Hotspurs cricket club. Their general love of sport saw them take up football at the end of 1882 to fill in the winter months, and on 30 September 1882, they played their first competitive match against another local side The Radicals, losing 2–0. Like a number of other local teams, The Hotspurs played their football on Tottenham Marshes, but they soon became the focus for groups of youngsters who were intent on disrupting the games. On more than one occasion, The Hotspurs were forced to defend their pitch from attack (possibly the first recorded pitch invasions?) and were finally forced to recruit the services of an adult both to run the club and to keep an eye on things.

By the end of the 1887–88 season, the club had changed its name to Tottenham Hotspurs to avoid confusion with the similarly named London Hotspurs. However, they had more pressing problems to deal with because their success and style of play were regularly drawing crowds of up to 4,000 down to the Marshes. They had already been forced to rope off the pitch to prevent intrusion onto the playing surface, but this did not stop either the verbal abuse or the throwing of mud and vegetables at opposing players by the crowd. Eventually, victims of their own success, the club were forced to move to Trulock Road just off Northumberland Park where they rented a pitch off a local tennis club. This enforced move had a plus side for the club, as they were finally able to charge entrance money to spectators, something that had been impossible on Tottenham Marshes as their pitch had been owned by the local council.

By the 1897–98 season, the club, now a member of the Football League and fully professional, were again suffering from over-crowding even at the new ground. Not only that, but among their support were a small unruly element bringing further problems. This came to a head when Spurs had their Northumberland Park ground closed for two weeks after their supporters attacked three

L*t*n Town players, who they blamed for the visiting club's appallingly poor tactics.

Later that same season, the continued overcrowding was almost responsible for a major disaster when, during a Good Friday game against local rivals Woolwich Arsenal, a crowd of over 14,000 squeezed into the tiny ground. In a quest for a better view, around 80 fans climbed onto the roof of a refreshment stand which promptly collapsed; thankfully, only five people were injured. With the club still increasing in size and attendance, this accident hastened the search for a new ground and at the end of the 1898–99 season, the club moved lock, stock and barrel to White Hart Lane.

As the club grew in stature, so did the attendances which, by the 1903–04 season, were regularly exceeding 20,000. It was during this season that the club was again hauled up before the authorities for the behaviour of its supporters. A mammoth crowd of almost 32,000 had crammed into the ground for an FA Cup tie against Aston Villa and the club had been forced to position benches around the pitch to help accommodate them. At half-time, with Spurs losing 1–0, those on the touchline got up and walked onto the pitch to stretch their legs. They were joined by thousands of others from the terraces and when the players came out for the second half, the crowd simply refused to leave the pitch, eventually forcing the referee to abandon the match. The FA were furious and fined Spurs £350 and ordered them to replay the game at Villa Park.

From this inauspicious start, the club grew into the major force it was eventually to become. However, unrest among the crowd was frequent, primarily when the club played their North London rivals Arsenal. Despite the fact that Spurs had moved to Highbury in 1916 to allow White Hart Lane to be used as a munitions factory for the remainder of the first world war, the two sets of fans never really got on and things came to a head in the twenties when the fans regularly fought outside the two grounds. Indeed, on one particular occasion, upwards of 100 men fought for some considerable time with iron bars and knives in the streets of Highbury.

In spite of these incidents, not just with Arsenal but with most of the clubs in the London area, Tottenham Hotspur had become one of the major forces in English football and by the early sixties, the North London club were pretty dominant in European competition as well. With trouble in the domestic game becoming almost routine, and Spurs fans being one of the major groups involved, it was to be only a matter of time before they seized the chance to travel abroad and cause trouble there. Although the sixties had seen a number of incidents involving English fans abroad, these mostly involved groups of servicemen and were nothing compared to what was to come. In 1974, Tottenham fans were to gain the dubious distinction of being the first English supporters to cause major disorder during a European fixture.

A UEFA Cup final against the Dutch side Feyenoord over two legs was always going to be hard work and with Tottenham drawing 2–2 at White Hart Lane, the team were faced with an uphill struggle in Rotterdam. The travelling fans, for their part, were intent on doing everything they could to support the team and travelled across the Channel in their thousands. For many of them, this was the first time they had left these shores and the availability of cheap alcohol fuelled the 'bulldog spirit' that was to become so prominent in the following years. Trouble had already erupted at a number of bars in the afternoon prior to the game and the police, completely unaware of how to deal with the problem, had adopted a high-profile stance in an effort to deter the fans from playing up.

Once inside the stadium, things were not that much better. Segregated from the opposing supporters by a simple chain-link fence, the Tottenham fans were making as much noise as possible in an effort to fire up the team, but things erupted when the referee disallowed what looked to the fans to be a perfectly legitimate goal. The Spurs supporters went for it in the biggest possible way, attacking rival fans and wrecking the away end. For the team, this almost certainly changed the game not only because they were visibly shocked at what was going on but also because the Spurs manager, Bill Nicholson, was forced to make a loudspeaker appeal at half-time when he should have been sorting out the tactics for the second half. Despite this, things did not improve, and a squad of baton-wielding riot police arrived and drove most of the Spurs fans out of the ground and into the surrounding streets, where the fighting continued for most of the evening. In the event, Spurs lost the game 2–0 on the night and 4–2 on aggregate, but with over 70 fans arrested and almost 200 injured, they had shamed both the club and the country.

Spurs were dragged up before UEFA and ordered to play their next two European home games 250 km from White Hart Lane, but as Spurs failed to qualify for another competition until 1980, this was never enforced. For Nicholson, this was the beginning of the end. His faith in the club and the love of the game were shaken by the events in Rotterdam and he quit Spurs four games into the next season.

In the domestic game the supporters continued to build on their reputation as being a major cause of disorder at games. The club were relegated to the second division at the end of the 1976–77 season and suddenly every game became a battle for the fans as the smaller clubs seized the opportunity to pit their wits against one of the big boys. The Spurs fans, strong in number and experienced battlers in their own right, began to mob up and take the fight to the opposition and made many fierce attacks on rival supporters when on their travels as Dave S. from Hove explained:

THE COCKEREL AND THE SEAGULLS

Word had got out that Tottenham were coming down to have a pop at Brighton because we'd had it away with some of their lads the last time we were in London and had given them a good running. Anyway, we thought we were more than ready and had everything planned to meet up on the Saturday morning and take them on the seafront where the police wouldn't be ready. Well, they caught us on the hop by coming down on the Friday night well mobbed-up and looking for it.

By all accounts, they got on the train in London and started wrecking it; then, when they arrived in Brighton, they steamed off and got into the town centre before the police knew what was happening. They found their way up to the Concorde, a restaurant in Madeira Drive, and tried to steam it, but because there was a private party or something they couldn't get in and it all went off. One of the doormen got the shit kicked out of him, but apparently the locals put up a good show. The coppers finally turned up and sorted it all. By then, though, word had got out and we were all pouring into the town to meet up and take them on.

It all went off later that night. At about one o'clock our main lads found them in West Street and chased them all over the place. We had loads of little mobs around the area as well, in Ship Street and Duke Lane, and they were picking off the stragglers. We gave them a right kicking and in the end they did a runner. I know some girl had her face smashed in with a brick really bad by one of them, broke her jaw I think, which was right out of order.

The next day, there were thousands of them at the game and it all went off again as word spread about the night before. Loads of missiles were being thrown around, which I didn't like. By then, the police were on top of it and after the game they got most of the Cockneys out of the town. Loads hung about, and it was kicking off right into the early hours before they finally pissed off back to London. Still, it was a right result for us though, I mean in those days Tottenham were a massive club and we had a real go at them.

The Spurs fans continued to cause mayhem wherever they went and, once promoted back to the First Division in 1978, had formed into a formidable group. Old scores were settled as the supporters made up for the missed season and although Tottenham never suffered from the same kind of stigma attached to either Chelsea or West Ham, their fans continued to cause trouble wherever they travelled. Like most clubs in the late seventies, every game was a potential trouble spot. Yet it was not to be until the early eighties that Spurs supporters were to come under the watchful gaze of the media again. Indeed, 1981 was to be a particularly rough time to be a Spurs fan.

At the FA Cup semi-final against Wolves in spring 1981, a scene took place that was to be a tragic pointer to future events. During the game Spurs fans became crushed into an enclosure behind one of the goals. The stewards, seeing that this was no ordinary crush and realising the dangers, opened the small gates and let the fans spill out onto the pitch. The ground concerned was Hillsborough. With the fans out of the pens, the stewards led them round to the Wolves end and put them in there with the result that a mass brawl broke out ending in numerous injuries and arrests. Later that same year, in November, a fan was killed during a fight involving Spurs and Manchester United supporters but if this was not bad enough, the club, having won the FA Cup, were to return to Holland for the first leg of the Cup-Winners' Cup. Their opponents, the mighty Ajax of Amsterdam.

As a result of their behaviour against Feyenoord only eight years previously, the Spurs fans were expecting a massive police presence for their visit and they were not disappointed. The reputation of English fans was at its lowest level – and falling. The police made it known that they would take no nonsense from anybody. They used undercover and plain-clothes officers, dogs, horses, commando police and even mobile sin-bins to control the Spurs fans, but of more relevance was the fact that it quickly became clear that the Dutch fans themselves were more than up for it.

Trouble began almost as soon as the Spurs supporters began arriving, and all over Amsterdam, particularly in the red-light district, Spurs fans were attacked and robbed by groups of Dutch fans. Indeed, mobs of Ajax fans up to 200 strong were wandering around the city centre looking for their English rivals. At the central railway station, a group of Spurs fans came under attack and, despite a concerted effort, three of them were stabbed and another thrown through a plate-glass window. The police accepted that it was not the Spurs fans' fault but still deported over 20 and hauled the rest up to the ground. In another incident, a mob of 60 Spurs fans fought a pitched battle with a large group of black youths resulting in yet more stabbings and over 20 Spurs fans were arrested. Again, UEFA was beside itself but apart from a slap on the wrists, nothing by way of punishment was handed out to either club. Yet the problems between Spurs and Dutch fans were clearly massive, and they weren't over yet.

At home, the Spurs fans soon found themselves with another problem, but this time it was totally unique. When Spurs qualified for the FA Cup semi-final against Leicester at Villa Park in 1982, their two Argentinian players – Ossie Ardiles and Ricky Villa – were the centre of media attention, especially as Villa had been the hero of the epic final against Manchester City the previous season. Tragically for him, Argentina invaded the Falklands on the eve of the game and the Leicester fans gave the two players some of the worst abuse ever heard at an English game. This led to serious problems outside the ground as the Spurs fans backed their players, even though the two nations were at war, something the Leicester fans took great exception to. With the country in shock at the events taking place in the South Atlantic, Ardiles returned to Argentina to play with the national side, while Villa was forced to stay in England and face the music. Because of this, the Spurs fans were subjected to intense aggression from opposing supporters, which only increased when some stated that they backed *their* players, as they were more important than anything else.

With Spurs winning the Leicester game and a Wembley appearance in front of them, Spurs were faced with a simple choice. Ardiles was unable to return from Argentina for the Cup final and it was clear that, in a diplomatic sense, Villa could hardly play a part in England's greatest sporting occasion with the two countries still at war. In the event, Spurs left Villa at home and he watched Tottenham's Cup final appearance, and the replay, on television but it signalled the end of his career in English football while Ardiles only returned to Spurs at a later date.

Two years later, Spurs, having failed miserably in the Cup-Winners' Cup the previous season, returned to the European stage via a fourth place in the league and it came as no surprise when the second round draw pitted them against their old foes, Feyenoord. With the events of Spurs' previous visits to Holland still fresh in the minds of many, not least the Spurs fans themselves, this was always going to be an intense occasion.

For once, the Dutch fans came to London for the first leg and caused a bit of trouble for the Metropolitan Police. The fact that they had shown at all was confirmation that the Dutch domestic game was catching up with the English as far as hooliganism was concerned. This trouble ensured that the return leg was going to be a dangerous trip for Spurs fans to make. Not only was it fairly certain that the Dutch police would be waiting for them, but it was also obvious that the Dutch fans would be waiting as well. The police once again adopted a wait-and-see approach, but made it plain that waiting in the wings were riot police, dogs and horses, and that they would all be called on if things got out of hand.

Sadly, the inevitable happened. Fighting broke out again early in the day and again inside the ground as the simmering trouble exploded primarily due to the fact that around 100 Spurs fans had purchased tickets in the middle of the Feyenoord section. Outside, in the streets of Rotterdam, things took a very nasty turn as the police struggled to keep on top of things and the trouble continued long into the evening. In the event, 30 people were seriously injured and Spurs were once again called up before UEFA and fined nearly £8,000.

Two years later, at the start of the 1986–87 season, Tottenham fans were on the back pages again, although this time it wasn't all down to them. No matter what the circumstances, any game that Glasgow Rangers play in England is of cause for concern because of the potential for trouble, and on this occasion, people were right to worry even though the game in question was a testimonial. The trouble started when a Rangers fan was found dead beside the tracks at Carlisle having apparently fallen out of the London-bound train. The police therefore had to detain and then interview numerous Rangers fans in London. This caused unrest among many of those Rangers fans already in the capital who were unaware of the circumstances and felt that the police were merely being heavy-handed. As a result, trouble started quite early, not only among the Rangers fans and the police, but also with the Spurs fans who were looking upon the game as an excuse to have a pop at the Scots as well as a large group of Chelsea fans who were attending the game as a result of their links with the Glasgow giants. More trouble erupted inside White Hart Lane leading, eventually, to fourteen arrests and a small number of policemen being put in hospital.

By this time, English clubs had been banned from Europe as a result of Heysel, but the Spurs fans continued to build on their reputation, not just because of trouble at their games but also through attacks on pubs and clubs all over the country. The sad fact of the matter was that this was a typical pattern at the time. Most games then saw trouble occur at some point, but by now the organised side of the burgeoning mob culture allied to football was kicking in. This was never more evident than at the 1987 FA Cup semi-final at Villa Park against our beloved Watford. Despite the intense atmosphere of the occasion the majority of the problems at the game did not involve the Hornets but another group of fans feared for their approach to football, Birmingham City's notorious Zulu Army.

ZULU TRIUMPH

Like most clubs at that time, Spurs used to think that they could come up to Birmingham and take the piss any time they liked and, like most of them, they ended up getting a right kicking. Spurs were no different, just a load of Cockney cunts who thought we were northern scum.

I've never understood why they played that game at Villa Park, I mean Watford's only up the road and surely Highbury would have been better. Anyway, when they said it would be played up here, we got in touch with their lads and arranged to meet up before the game and sort things out once and for all.

For an occasion like this, it wasn't hard to rustle up a decent mob and in all we must have pulled in about 300 lads who were all certainly able to look after themselves. At about ten o'clock, we were all ready and tooled-up and travelled over to where we had arranged to have it away which was, like most of our battles, outside a pub. As soon as we got near, we split into two so that we could hit them from both sides. We could see that they had about 40 lads outside waiting for us. As soon as they saw us, we steamed down towards them and went straight in and kicked it all off. They came at us with pool balls, cues and bottles, but we managed to force them back into the pub as the second lot came steaming in from the other side. That really fucked them up because they obviously thought that the first attack was our main mob, not just half of it! We smashed our way into the pub through the windows and it really went off. I've only ever been in anything like that once before, and that was against Man United at New Street Station but at least there you could move, inside that pub it was just rammed and everyone was at it. After about ten minutes of this, we started to hear sirens as the police came steaming in and as we pulled out to do a runner, it was obvious that someone had been at it with blades. I saw at least one Spurs lad in a pool of blood, but some of our lot said a couple more had been spiked, although we didn't know who had done it. Well, once the police were in, we did the off and left them to it. Three hundred lads had been in, kicked the shit out of them, and not one got arrested.

By the early nineties, Spurs fans were suffering from a new problem, one that had nothing to do with hooliganism but everything to do with the club. The early eighties had seen the club come under the control of a board headed by Irving Scholar, who decided that the time was right to float the club on the stock exchange. Some fans felt this sent out a message that the club didn't belong to them anymore. This initially led to a great deal of resentment from the supporters but as things appeared to take shape, it looked as if the club were indeed on the up. The board began pouring money into the ground and also set out on a course of commercialisation aimed at bringing in more money to strengthen the team. In principle this was fine, but it still missed the essential point: most of the money for the club came from one source – the fans – and all of this was happening with little consultation with them. The early resentment returned and the anger directed at the board became intense. The sports equipment company Hummel set up by Tottenham Hotspur PLC failed and by the early nineties, the club was having to consider selling some of its star players in an attempt to clear the massive debt it now found itself stuck with. It was a tough time for the club, talks with Robert Maxwell took place but eventually, Terry Venables and Alan Sugar bought the club and set out to rescue them from the threat of bankruptcy. Even so Paul Gascoigne was still sold to Lazio, which didn't please the majority of the fans.

Like most clubs at the time, Tottenham and its supporters were shocked by the events at Hillsborough. The shockwaves that reverberated through the English game ensured that in most cases, the hooligan groups went quiet for a time and Spurs were no exception. However, this did not stop the odd bit of trouble taking place and a number of towns saw Spurs fans indulge in the sort of mayhem that was becoming less and less frequent.

With the Premier League in full swing and the changes enforced on the game by the Taylor Report, the Tottenham fans went a bit quiet for a while, something they had in common with most clubs. The growing use of CCTV and the threats that went along with it worked well within White Hart Lane and trouble inside the ground became almost unknown. The potential for trouble in the streets around grounds continued and Spurs fans were involved in incidents at numerous games over the following seasons although there were few major problems.

But, in March 1993, this was all to change as the bad, old days returned. During an FA Cup quarter-final tie at Maine Road, Manchester City fans invaded the pitch three minutes from the end of the game following a late goal. The trouble was that they didn't want to leave the pitch as the invasion turned into an apparent attempt to get the game called off. Billy C. from Manchester takes up the story:

MAINE ROAD TO MAIN LINE

Once we were on the pitch, the word quickly spread that we were staying on to try to get the game called off. We were 4–2 down with no time left to get back in and we wanted another chance, simple as that. It was nothing to do with the Spurs really. There'd been a bit outside the ground but that was just normal stuff; this was different. After about five minutes, the police came steaming in trying to get us off but we just spread out, broke ranks and went round them, it was comical really. Then they brought on the horses and it all changed. I hate those things – they're bloody lethal – and they had something like twelve or thirteen of them out on the pitch. That was that, we were off but the mood was different then, we were all pissed off.

Once the game finished, the Spurs fans were giving it all the usual mouth and it was obvious then that it was going to go off outside. The police must have thought that we had calmed down a bit, because there hadn't been any trouble on the pitch, so I don't think they were expecting anything, but they got a bit of a shock. We didn't hang around outside the ground, but all the lads went directly to Piccadilly station because we knew that a good number of their lads had come up by train and the railway is always a good place for an off because once the police get them away, that's the end of it and they leave us alone.

Well, once they turned up, it kicked off straight away and there was some manic stuff. They certainly had a go back and for a time it looked as though they might have got a result but as more lads arrived, we managed to force them down onto the platforms. There were loads of missiles flying around before the police got their act together and got between us. After that it was all the usual stuff, loads of shouting and verbal but we had made our point. That was good enough.

The events at this game seemed to have been something of a

catalyst for the Spurs mob, because after the Man City game they seemed to have discovered a taste for trouble. Certainly the semi-final clash against Arsenal at Wembley was littered with clashes between the two sets of fans all over North London.

As the Premier League continued to grow in stature, the activities of Spurs supporters continued unabated. Clashes with all the London clubs were routine and, on the road, trouble occurred almost everywhere they went. It wasn't that major and often it was initiated by opposition fans wanting to have a pop at a London club. This was particularly true when Spurs visited Bolton, whose fans are hardly renowned for their hospitality in any case. Spurs supporters, and not just the fighting lads, found themselves on the receiving end of some particularly aggressive behaviour from the Northerners. There is certainly a strong possibility of revenge being taken when Bolton return to the Premiership in 1997.

This latest incident, however, merely confirmed that Spurs fans had a small but growing reputation in the hooligan field.

The violent elements at Tottenham are not known for getting themselves that well organised at home matches, but this horrific account might make you think twice when heading to this part of North London.

SPURS V COVENTRY

Last season, for the first time in my life, I felt like I would never go to football again after witnessing the worst thing I'd ever seen in my life. Before our last match down at White Hart Lane, word had gone out that our lads were going down mobbed-up to have a go at the Spurs lads. We've always had problems with Spurs, they are one of the worst London clubs as far as we are concerned. They seem to know the pubs and places to hit and always turn out when they come here, so I think the feeling was to make a bit of a showdown at their place for once.

I went down by train with a couple of mates, and to look at us you would think we were your typical footy thugs. I like to wear good gear and look the part, and I like the odd spot of bother, but I suppose I'm one of those blokes on the edge of it all, the type who is last in when it looks like we're going to get a result. We're not part of the mob.

After a few drinks near Euston, we made our way up to the ground and went to the usual pub about half a mile away. There are always a few Sky Blues in there and we got talking to a few lads sitting outside. I've never been one for wearing the colours as I remember seeing too many slaps given out by City and other fans, but these lads had their shirts on and, to tell the truth, nine times out of ten you can get away with that nowadays. They had been in the pub for an hour or so, and said they hadn't seen or heard of any trouble and didn't expect anything to happen.

We had been drinking there for about half an hour when this group of about twelve lads came walking up on the other side of the road. I could see straightaway that they looked like the type, all dressed up, strutting along and buzzed up. As they crossed the road, I told my mates to have a look and watch their backs. You could tell they were ready to go. For a moment it looked like they were going straight past us, but as they got level, they all pulled stuff out of their pockets and started lashing out. They were carrying these little squeezy bottles, like Vicks nasal sprays, and squirted them at our faces. A couple of lads went down holding their eyes and they were on them right away. They were like animals, screaming their heads off and offering everyone out. A couple of lads went for it, but they were flashing the knives in front of us and we soon backed off. No one wanted any of that shit. They kept screaming, 'Where's your boys, where's your fucking boys?' One of the lads on the floor had taken a right hiding, and as the lads at the front kept waving the knives and shouting at us, the ones at the back kept sticking the boot in. There were a couple of Spurs lads from in the pub that had come out. When they saw the state of the lad on the floor, they pleaded with this mob to stop and said that they had done enough.

The landlord had called the police, so they did a runner up the road and disappeared.

I went over to see how this lad was, but one of his mates was shouting to get an ambulance as he was losing a lot of blood and unconscious. He was holding a beer towel to his face but you could see already it was soaked in blood. When he took it away, I saw his face. He had been cut right down the side, from above his ear to below his bottom lip. His cheek was flapped open and you could see right inside. The blood was pouring out. Really, he was lucky to be out cold as it would probably have freaked him out. I had never seen anything like it and I felt sick. Three minutes earlier, he had been enjoying a quiet pre-match drink with his mates. That could have been any one of us, it could have been me lying there with half my face hanging off.

The police arrived well before the ambulance. When they turned up, they started off by giving it the large one, but the Tottenham fans soon told them what had happened and they changed just like that. Some of the City fans were having a go at the police about finding these animals, really going mad. The ambulance turned up and took the lad away, and the police offered us an escort to the ground. They wanted statements and everything, so they took our names and two of the City lads went with the police to see if they could spot the Spurs lads in the crowd from the cameras.

The police said they were expecting trouble because the Spurs nutters were expecting City to turn up in numbers, but they hadn't. That was why when the police turned up, they did so in numbers because they thought we were the City firm they had been looking for.

I went to the match but, looking back on it, I must have been in shock. Everyone was talking about this poor lad. At half-time I went up to a steward and asked him if I could leave. I just wanted to be away from there. The next thing I knew, I was sitting on a train back to Coventry looking out of the window all on my own. I didn't even tell my mates I was going. They were worried sick, and had a right go at me as they had spent most of the second half looking for me. Eventually they had told a steward I was missing and found out that I had left.

I can see that lad's face whenever I shut my eyes. I am back going to football now, after staying away for a few games, but I won't go to an away game. I know the streets around here, where to go and where not to go, so I feel fairly safe. I still think, though, that could have been me being battered by those bastards.

By 1996, violence at football throughout England had settled into a sadly predictable pattern. The supporters of the Premier League clubs continued their activities out of the public eye while those of the smaller clubs went at it in the same old fashion, although few noticed. This all began to change during the build-up to Euro 96 when the whole issue of hooliganism was thrown back into the public eye. Despite the FA and media campaign designed to fool Joe Public into thinking everything was rosy, Spurs fans were among those implicated in trouble and a number of their following were arrested in dawn raids after serious trouble with both Arsenal and Chelsea the previous season. This proved conclusively that the club's fans were being regarded as major players in the hooliganism stakes, and during the 1996–97 season trouble erupted at both the Wolves and Hereford FA Cup ties, and the Nottingham Forest and Aston Villa league games.

For Spurs as a club, the future continues to look a bit ropey. The obvious unrest among the fans at the Alan Sugar regime has caused friction between the board and the supporters. The distinguished history of the club means its fans almost demand success, and that is simply not happening. Unless the situation is resolved, then the potential for protest and trouble could well develop further, as has been seen all too often at a number of clubs. As regards the hooligan element at Tottenham, it is difficult to work out exactly what the future holds for them. While they have never really 'enjoyed' the reputation of certain other London clubs, or been rated by rival mobs, it is clear that they command a grudging respect. That respect has been earned through season after season of confrontation, though it is not clear that the supporters actually want to live up to this reputation.

As one of the North London giants, the traditional support for Tottenham always, fairly obviously, came from that area. This was helped in the early years by the fact that White Hart Lane was in the centre of Tottenham and was easily accessible via the Seven Sisters Road and the growing tube network. However, following the second world war, and in common with the other London clubs, large sections of this support left London and moved out of the city into the new towns surrounding the capital. Suddenly towns such as Welwyn Garden City, Stevenage and Hemel Hempstead found themselves with large groups of Spurs fans who regularly travelled to watch their club.

As the seasons passed, some of those exiles formed small mobs of men more than willing and able to stand and fight and so the club soon became renowned for having loads of small mobs rather than one massive one. In some ways, this has been the reason why the club has never suffered from the stigma attached to Millwall, West Ham or Chelsea because the lack of one single hooligan group has not provided a target for the media to latch onto. Yet within those mobs are a number of individuals who rank among some of the worst hooligans in the country. If you look back at the events surrounding Spurs trips into Europe, and Holland in particular, it is clear that when these mobs get together they make a formidable firm and it does make us wonder what would happen if they were ever to get it together on a weekly basis. Yet while these separate groups exist, it is strange that not more is heard of them, or that they do not adopt the type of name so beloved of many of their opposing groups. While the fans who watched their football from the sadly long-gone Shelf were always held in high regard as a fighting group, we have only ever heard of two firms allied to Spurs adopting names: the N17s, named after the postal code of White Hart Lane and the Yids or Yiddos, a name derived from the commonly held, but inaccurate, belief that Spurs have a massive Jewish following. The most likely reason for this myth is that the areas close to Tottenham have historically contained a large Jewish element. Yet those of the Jewish faith who do go to games are just as likely to go to Arsenal as Spurs. However, one benefit of this reputation is that it has ensured that racial abuse, so obvious at many other London clubs, has remained thankfully absent at the Lane, and all who care to look will notice that Tottenham are lucky enough to enjoy great support from most of the minority groups.

While most London clubs have problems with Spurs, or vice versa depending on your loyalties, the big one for all Tottenham fans is, of course, Arsenal. As we have already mentioned, the two sets of fans were fighting each other back in the twenties but even that was some way down the line as fighting had been reported when the two teams met in 1898, the year the refreshment bar roof collapsed at Northumberland Park.

Strangely, neither the time spent ground-sharing at Highbury during the first world war, nor having Arsenal play at White Hart Lane during the second world war saw any trouble involving supporters, probably because most of the male population were otherwise engaged. However, over the seasons, the number of incidents between the two sets of fans could fill a book such as this and it would make for very uncomfortable reading. Attacks at pubs and clubs, on the railway, on the tube network and even at motorway service stations were, and sadly often are, commonplace. Even pre-arranged confrontations are not uncommon. The debut of Jurgen Klinsmann for Spurs at Watford was notable for the lack of serious trouble, but this was due to the fact that the main Spurs lads were elsewhere, a 'meeting' between them and Arsenal elsewhere being far too important to back out of. Ironically, when they came to Vicarage Road later in the season for a Cup game, trouble was bubbling over everywhere. It also became clear that Spurs fans were at the forefront of trouble in and around London during Euro 96, and this came as something of a surprise to many. The rumoured link-up between the hooligan mobs from the London clubs never occurred, and Spurs and Chelsea fans fought with each other on at least two occasions in the West End. Certainly the trouble outside the Porcupine on the night of the Scotland game involved Spurs fans, and they came in for a great deal of criticism from within the hooligan world for their actions, as most believed that all efforts should have been directed at the Scottish supporters in Trafalgar Square.

Yet the reputation of the Spurs fighting fans is a growing one. As mentioned already, the number of incidents involving Tottenham fans is on the increase and it is certain that the police are keeping a wary eye on them. It may well be a good idea for the rest of us to do so as well. Tottenham, never a team to be taken lightly, have a minority of their supporters who demand the same attention from the rest of us.

Every now and again, football provides the supporter with a memory that will live long in the telling. This account of a visit to Spurs comes from Steve W. and must go down with the best.

BUMS, BRIDES AND ROLLERSKATES

We had travelled down to London on a coach hired by the landlord of the local for a Cup match at White Hart Lane against Spurs. We had been on the ale all day and were well pissed-up, singing our heads off and making the most of our big day out, when the bus turned into this main high street. The traffic was rammed and we were moving at a snail's pace when we started to pass a wedding in full swing. The bride, groom, bridesmaids, the lot, were all lined-up on the steps of the church having the wedding photos taken, so some of the lads started giving the bride all the usual shit. You know, 'Get your tits out for the lads', etc, etc. They all tried to ignore it as best they could, but then some lads started to drop their trousers and do moonies at them. All the kids were laughing and the bride was starting to get upset, which of course only made it worse for her. This bloke walks over and does his best to get us to have some respect, which made it funnier and funnier as they dug themselves a deeper hole. Then out of the blue, this black guy goes past on rollerskates looking like a complete prat. He was done up like a Christmas tree in one of those really loud shellsuits, wearing a massive floppy hat, strutting down the street and dancing away to the music he could hear on his headphones. Suddenly all the verbal gets directed at him.

Once he realised all the verbal was aimed at him, he pulled off the headphones, listened to the verbal then walked to the front of the bus. He whacked the emergency-door button and got on, as the whole bus went quiet. 'What's your problem?' Still quiet. 'I said, what's your problem? You're not so mouthy now then, eh?' Then someone shouts back, 'Mate, what have you come as?' The bus erupted. Then someone else shouted, 'Get off our bus, you wanker.' That was it, he went mental.

'Come on then, you get off the bus and I'll kick your arse back to where you came from, come on!' He was gesturing for someone to get off, but no one fancied it. Everyone was shouting back at him to fuck off the bus, when he walks up the aisle and lumps one of the lads. Now it has to be said that he had a lot of bottle to do what he did, but that don't do you any good if you're as thick as shit, because that was a bad move. Everyone went piling over the seats, trying to get a punch in but mostly punching each other more than anything else. The bus was rocking from side to side, and the wedding party looked on as it turned out to be more of a mass bundle than a fight. The poor sod got rolled back down the aisle and off the bus, ending up by the side of the road, dazed and minus one rollerskate. He didn't know where he was.

We moved off laughing our heads off when suddenly the police turn up mob-handed and pile on the bus. Once again we sit there, 50 pissed-up lads, all quiet and looking all angelic. With one story against 50 there wasn't much they could do really, except take the rollerskater away and calm him down. Once they had made their point and shown us who was boss, they then escorted us to the ground to avoid any further trouble – and got us the best parking space at the same time!

PART SEVEN
Capital Teams

Chapter 15
London Fields

In this section, we take a brief look at the other clubs within the capital and the exploits of their hooligan fans. We should start by pointing out that you could probably write a book on every firm in the country, but unfortunately we only have so much space and can only write what we have been told and know to be true. Many fans will be none too happy with this because everyone likes to think their lads are the top boys, but we do not pretend to be writing the history of every firm. Admittedly in this book we have concentrated on the big three – Chelsea, Millwall and West Ham – because they have been the most active. However, as we have stated in our previous books, every club (and we mean *every* club) has a few lads that can, and often will, cause serious problems.

As we have seen, the tube network is one of the greatest weapons the London football hooligans have at their disposal. Every London side has had its moments on the underground, ambushing unsuspecting fans from all over the country as well as their local rivals. There is one firm in particular that has used the tube continually over the years to surprise the opposition. This story has been told to us over and over again by supporters who have suffered the same ambush, on the same tube line, by what would appear to be the same small but extremely violent firm.

* * *

QPR TUBE

We had been up the West End as normal, doing a bit of shopping and having a few beers. We hooked up with some other lads in the Globe pub then, after a few more bevvies, caught the tube down to Shepherd's Bush. I've never liked the tube, but there were a few of us and the beer had taken away most of the fear. We were singing and generally being a pain in the arse for all the other passengers when the train pulled into Ladbroke Grove station. The doors opened and these lads jumped on. There were only about ten of them but they were buzzing like fuck. There is nothing like another mob appearing from nowhere to sober you up. The doors shut and we were trapped in together.

They were mad for it, really raging. We were keeping well quiet, then they started sussing the carriage out. 'Come on, then. Where's the northern cunts? Come on. We're fucking Rangers, Rangers. Come on, who wants it?' They were all well tooled-up, carrying those hand-rests that hang from the ceiling. They were right in everyone's face, including ours. As soon as someone opened their mouth we were dead. Then this little bastard grassed us up. They went fucking mad and had us pinned up on the end. All of a sudden, a couple of the lads started screaming and I could smell bleach or something. They had Jif lemon bottles full of something and were squirting it into our faces. The lads that had been sprayed started to panic and I don't blame them, it could have been anything for all they knew. I just curled up on the floor, but a few of the lads had tried to fight back as there was nowhere to go. We pulled into the next stop, the door opened and off they went, as quick as they came on.

We were left battered and bruised and well fucked-off. The grass had got off as well, which was a good job because he would have got the kicking of his life if he'd stayed on.

I have to congratulate them, it was a great hit, well sorted.

I'll only use the tube if we're well mobbed-up now. I wouldn't mind meeting that lot again, but only if we had the same armoury as they had.

Supporting Crystal Palace must be a very frustrating hobby. The club can call on large numbers of support when things are going well, yet unfortunately they do suffer from a lack of publicity as the team have never seemed to reach their full potential. As far as their hooligan following is concerned, they are another side that can turn out a very tidy firm when the need arises. Unlike most other London firms, they do not have a history of using the tube network to their advantage, perhaps because they're so far from the nearest tube station, but seem happier on their own patch. We have spoken to many hooligans throughout the country and were surprised to hear that they rated Palace more highly than many of the better-known firms.

Tony from Croydon supplied the following account of an away day at one of their main rivals.

OH, WE DO LIKE TO BE BESIDE THE SEASIDE

Any match down at Brighton is a big game for the lads, and we had a pre-season friendly down there in 1993 which went right off. Why they kept playing this fixture I don't know, because the season before we had played them as well and it was well naughty. I would have thought the police would have put a stop to it.

A lot of the lads had taken the afternoon off work, so we mobbed-up in the local then got the train down at three o'clock. There were no Brighton lads around at the time so we went off on a pub crawl. The trouble with Brighton is that it's full of drop-outs and benders, so finding a decent pub wasn't that easy and we ended up doing the rounds before making our way to the Prince George pub, where we had arranged to meet all the late-comers. As time went on, we slowly grew in numbers and managed to empty the pub of most of the low-life. The landlord was having a right result for a Tuesday afternoon, so he wasn't too upset at us pissing his regulars off.

At about six o'clock, a group of about six or seven lads turned up and said that there were a few Brighton boys keeping an eye on the station. These Palace lads had been chased but an Old Bill van had shot down the road after the locals and that had put a stop to it. As soon as you hear something like that, the old adrenaline starts to buzz. It went around the pub like wild-fire and everyone started to hang onto their empties, to be tucked into jacket pockets for later.

The Old Bill hadn't cottoned on to us yet, but now the lads were starting to get more vocal and a few were starting to move outside. Then the door opened and we got the nod that there were a few lads starting to scout the place out. Most of us moved outside to join the others, then the Albion lads showed up. There were about 40 of them in all, closely followed by the Bill who then saw us for the first time and quickly tried to get in between us.

We started giving each other the verbal then they made the first move when a bottle came flying over. The cheer went up as lads from both mobs moved forward, and all hell broke loose. They were well-prepared and as the missiles flew through the air, most of our lads were forced back in the pub. The Old Bill bottled it and left us to it. I did the off down the road and the Brighton lads went for the pub. First, this guy grabbed this bike and put it through the window. As all their boys stood back, this other lad came forward and lobbed a CS gas canister into the pub.

It's horrible having to watch your lads getting ambushed, but we were in no-man's land as there were only five of us and we would have got slaughtered. There was about 30 seconds' silence then all our lads came piling out of the pub to escape the gas. The Brighton lads steamed in again, along with the Old Bill who finally got involved. I saw one of my mates on the floor getting kicked to fuck. We started to move up as a few of our lads were back with it and hitting back. Then we heard the police sirens and all the Brighton lads did the off, coming straight towards us. We stopped in our tracks. As they got nearer, some started to slow and look as if they were nothing to do with it. They were full of themselves and we wanted a result here. As the last few got level with us, my mate smacked this lad right across the nose with this metal bar he had nicked from the train. He went straight down and as they moved back, we all pulled our tools out to keep them back. As one moved forward, my mate waved a blade at him as he stood over this lad on the floor and shouted for them to come forward if they wanted slicing. They stood off and as the lad on the floor came round, he got a few kicks before I lobbed the bottle I had at his head. It bounced off without breaking but he would have a nasty cut from that. The Old Bill came in at the top of the road and the Brighton lads did the runner. The pub was mobbed with Old Bill; like wankers, they had steamed into the pub without thinking and a couple of them were knocked out by the gas. We walked up to join the rest of the lads who were now surrounded by the brave old bobby, who was totally in control of the situation – like fuck. At first they even thought we were the ones who had gassed the pub!

It was a good hit by the Brighton lads but this wasn't over by a long way, our lads were going garrity. The coppers didn't arrest anyone and escorted us to the ground. During the match, we could spot most of their lads from the pub. They were giving it the large one and it was clear they wanted more after as well. The Old Bill were everywhere now. Fuck knows where they all come from, but you wouldn't have had much joy if your house had been burgled in Brighton that night.

We were mobbed-up to about 80 lads now and they looked to be getting the numbers up as well. Just before the final whistle they all did the off, so we knew they would be trying something. It's usually the same old tactic, walk up the hill to the corner of the park and then steam down. You'd think that the local coppers would have sussed this by now, but I've known them to use this at least four times. True to form, there they were but in good numbers, about 150.

They kicked it off with a few bricks being lobbed over, but this time we were straight in. A lot of their lads did the off, but a fair few had the bottle to fight it out and, along with the coppers getting involved, this was a top row. We finally got on top and steamed them down past their end, followed by the cry of 'Eagles, Eagles'. That's fucking lovely, running a mob on their own manor.

The coppers got between us and forced our lot back against the wall. We'd been waiting there for about five minutes when the Brighton mob came back again, lobbing stones and anything else they could get their hands on. The coppers charged at them and that was it, they had gone. We were walked down to Hove station and put on a train that was waiting for us. Brighton station was well noisy as we sung our hearts out. The Old Bill made sure that we couldn't get off at the next stop and come back in, by holding up one of the fast trains that doesn't stop until it reaches Croydon.

For Charlton Athletic, all the coming and going between The Valley, Selhurst Park and then back to The Valley had a major effect on their fan base and, along with that, the hooligan element. John from Welling explains how this nomadic existence affected him.

OUT OF THE VALLEY

I feel sorry for the lads that follow football today. I don't think they will ever experience the excitement of being part of a firm in the way that me and my mates did, because football has become so watered down. Football then was full-on, the atmosphere was electric at the derby games. Palace, West Ham, Millwall, it was madness. You knew it would go off, you knew that there would be Chelsea in your end, but where they were and when it would kick off kept you buzzing. Who was the bloke next to you? Were those five blokes up at the tea bar West Ham or not? It was fucking great. Spotting people as they came in, and that feeling when you both twigged who was who – amazing.

You knew you couldn't do the likes of Chelsea but you would always put up a show, and if you could put the boot in then that would keep you going for years down the pub. If you came out with a lump on the head or, even better, had blood on you, then it showed that you were there and up for it. Like it or not, in those days people loved it and respected you for it; not now.

Now, when I go down The Valley, I don't recognise anyone. The place is full of mums, kids and people I've never seen before. Not so long ago, on one of the few occasions that I go nowadays, I was asked at the gate who I supported – I wasn't part of it anymore, it didn't know me and I didn't belong; the football club had become bollocks. I followed that club for over 20 years and knew everyone that was anyone, from the players down to the tea lady, and they all knew who and what I was.

Moving to Selhurst Park was one thing, but it was the move back to The Valley that really made me sit up and take notice. Like everyone else, I did all I could to get the club back where it belonged. I marched, posted leaflets, made phone calls – some nice, some not so nice – and hassled anyone that had any influence on the final decision. When we won, we went mad and had the biggest piss-up you could imagine, it was a fantastic time. The first few games were pretty good as they were more like parties than football matches. It was then that I should have realised what was going on.

The club had been busy marketing the new Valley to the family audience. This was their chance to rid the club of the small, but visible, violent few that they had been saddled with for years. The pats on the back for all the help and campaigning were soon replaced with looks over the shoulder, no more free tickets from the players (a club directive, we were told) and no more post-match drinks with the lads either, because the club needed to clean up its image within the community, a community of which we were a part, and still are.

For me, the thing that totally killed it was the seats. We would go, the usual 20 or so, find our place as close as we could to our original terrace spot, sing, shout and stand around looking like a firm did, always on the scout for visiting lads and generally letting people know who we were. Then people started to complain: they didn't like the 'aggressive' gestures to visiting players and fans, the swearing was upsetting their birds! Even the singing, for fuck's sake, was annoying people because we would stand up and it would spoil their view. I mean, what is football all about these days?

Things started to get a bit heavy and the odd punch was being exchanged, so the club started to post stewards all around us and the police filmed our every move. If more than three of us went to get a cup of tea together, a steward would follow. It was pathetic and all done to wind us up. For a while it all became a game. When something happened on the pitch, like a players' punch-up, the rest of the crowd would be going mad and we would try our hardest to stay calm as though nothing was happening. That foxed them a bit at times. The stewards and the police would try to strike up a conversation, being all matey, but we wouldn't say a word back. We even managed to stay seated once when we scored which, looking back, was bollocks because we weren't supporting the team; the whole thing had become a total joke.

Then one day, when one of the lads was at the club shop, he bumped into the stadium manager and was asked in for a 'chat'. He was asked what our problem was and why wouldn't we just move over to be with the rest of the fans that wanted to sing? He told my mate that they had us by the balls now because they could monitor our every move and isolate us, and he was right, of course. My mate told him to fuck off, got up and walked out. From then on, things just got worse.

Away games were different. If any Charlton fan said anything we would go mental, we were having more run-ins with our own fans than the other team's, but eventually

I had had enough. It was costing a fortune, the football was shit, wasn't worth the hassle and, worst of all, I found myself hating the club I had once loved – something I never could have dreamed would happen.

There are still a few lads that go and I get reports of the odd off, but it's not done the same way. You don't get to defend your territory in the way that we did. I ain't saying that the lads that go now ain't up for it, either: society has become much more violent over the last ten years so I am sure they can more than handle themselves, but we had it week after week.

I still follow Charlton but only go at Christmas and Cup games. If I go to a game now, I go to Welling along with a few of the other lads. There's more chance of an off there than at Charlton, sometimes it gets really nasty. We haven't got involved, yet, we just have a pint in the club bar, talk about the old days and watch the results on telly. When Charlton win there's a bigger cheer in the bar than when Welling score. Funny, that.

When the Valiants do have a major fixture, they can also find themselves with a major turn-out from the old faces. When the opposition have a reputation for mixing it with the best, then the numbers looking for some action can be even greater still, as Mr M. told us.

CUP FEVER

In 1994 we were drawn to play Bristol City up at their place in the fifth round of the FA Cup. This was a big game, one of those matches where all the old faces turn out for the crack, and the club had no trouble in selling all the 5,000 tickets they had given us. With that many travelling, there is always going to be a fair few lads ready to have a go if things kick off, and Bristol are known to have a good mob.

The night before the match, I was drinking with some Spurs fans and they said they knew of some other Yids who were going up to the game just to have it away with the locals. Spurs and City had a meeting in London the previous season and this was an extension of that. He had also heard that some Millwall and Chelsea lads were going, as they had also had trouble with the Bristol firm over the last couple of seasons.

We went by minibus and all the way down we were passing coach after coach of Charlton fans having the crack. It must have been the biggest following we had taken anywhere for ages. When we arrived, we were put in a car park with all the other buses. There must have been at least 50 of them and Charlton were everywhere.

We went into the Robins for a drink and the place was packed with Charlton. Over in the corner, keeping themselves to themselves, were a small group of lads I didn't know, but they all had London accents so we started having a rabbit. They told us they were Tottenham and that there were also some Chelsea lads about as well. What my mate had told me wasn't bollocks after all: they had come down for the row.

All the talk was about fighting and by the time we left the pub we were pumping. That was the first we saw of the City lads; loads of little mobs at first, then they came together and had a go at the Old Bill as things started to get a bit vocal.

In our end we were all split up, as the tickets allocated a section of the ground and the stewards were sticking to it. That's bollocks, it causes more problems than it solves, as lads get angry and you get little pockets of lads playing up rather than one big one.

All the City lads were sitting up in the top tier, really baiting us. Then they scored. As they went mental, it went off in the far corner as both sets of fans tried to climb the fencing. Loads more police arrived and that kept things quiet, even after we scored and secured a replay.

As it got towards the end of the game, large sections of the City fans were getting up to leave all at once. These were their main lads and I am not talking about 30 blokes, more like groups of 200: they were getting together big numbers. This was starting to look dodgy as we were all split up by the ticket arrangement and would be going out in small groups rather than mobbed-up. We came out of the ground and were facing the big park that was behind the away end then. There were no police or stewards around at all. Then we heard the shout go up and they came steaming down the hill at us, fucking hundreds of them. All there was to keep us apart was a piece of rope! The Bristol lads must have used this tactic loads of times because as we turned to face them, more came out from behind some advertising hoardings to the side and steamed us from there. They didn't give a fuck who they hit out at: women, old men, didn't matter. They were nutty.

We had to fight it out, there was nowhere to go – and slowly we got the numbers up to stand our ground. Then all of a sudden the B Mob, Charlton's main lads, appeared and things were more even, with both lots having their moments. The place was like a battleground. The police came flying in and nicked anyone they could get their grubby hands on. If they had been there in the first place, it wouldn't have gone off – tossers.

On the day, we stood our ground, we didn't run and that's the main thing. Bristol are supposed to have one of the top firms in the country and little old Charlton had stood and battled it out with them: result. It goes to show that, at the end of the day, it doesn't matter if there are a thousand of you, if a few run then loads follow – but if fifty of you stand, then others will soon join and you are likely to come out with your reputation intact.

The replay went off quietly, although there were hundreds of Old Bill there to soon stop it if it had kicked off, and we won 2–0.

Cardiff fan Nick explains that not every firm views a trip to the capital with apprehension. Read on.

HAVING A WALES OF A TIME

London is always a top day out for the Soul Crew. It's not just about being Bluebirds but about being Welsh as well. I hate the English, and the Cockneys in particular: mouthy, flash bastards too quick to pull the knives out.

We will always have a scout around the West End, you know, Soho and Covent Garden and visit the top clothes shops like the Armani shop on Brompton Road. We like to let people know we're there, so we'll find a pub, take it over and have a good sing-song and wait to see if any other mob wants to pay us a visit. It may not only be the London firms you come across – I remember a big row with some Stoke lads a while back. They're a tidy mob, Stoke.

With the club being so crap we never get to play the top teams, just the likes of Fulham, Orient, Barnet and Brentford, but the great thing about London is that these smaller clubs usually have some lads from other teams ready to join them, so usually we do get to see some action.

In '88 we went down to Orient and caused mayhem. Chelsea and West Ham were playing that day, so we were looking to meet them as well. This brought out everyone as there had been a big recruitment drive in Cardiff in the build-up to the big day. As we took such a large number, it was sure to go off before the game finished, which ruined the meet with the big boys. But some of the West Ham lads had turned up at the Orient match and they put up a good show. These smaller clubs have their lads as well, it wasn't all West Ham. On the final whistle, we invaded the pitch and chased up to the home lads, running them out of the ground. Outside, they were a bit better organised and had a go back, but once we were mobbed-up they had no chance really. The Met are always ready to wade in and bust a few heads, they don't mind a bit of a fight themselves; really nasty, that lot. There was plenty of trouble on the tube and the police saw us straight back to Paddington station, which turned out lovely because we met up with some Newport County lads and battered the fuck out of them as well. We ran riot at Paddington that day, there were people running everywhere. That's what's so good about London: it can kick off time after time.

When we went to Barnet a few seasons later we did much the same thing, only this time we got the game stopped for about ten minutes when we invaded the pitch to get at a mob of Arsenal lads that had come down to have a go. I don't think they really knew what to expect from us, but they soon found out. At Enfield in the FA Cup, it was meant to be the Spurs lads coming to have a go and there was a lot of fighting in the high street after that match. Cup games are always good for a scrap.

I think one of the main reasons that no one invests money in the club is because of the violent following we have. I mean, this club should be massive. As soon as we start putting it together, the crowds go right up – but along with that, so does the amount of head-cases. I don't think there is a club in Britain that has such a big percentage of supporters ready to get involved if it kicks off. I hate to think what it would be like if we were playing Chelsea, Liverpool and Man United every week. We'd be banned from everywhere.

When we went to Fulham in August '93, the club were on the up and the away support was massive. Fulham have a reputation for linking up with Chelsea for big games. We had already caused trouble at Blackpool and Port Vale and the trip to London was going to be the next big day out for the Soul Crew. We had scouted the West End as normal and rumours kept coming back that Chelsea were out for us. We left it late to arrive at the ground, as this sometimes fucks the police off and you can get in for nothing. But the Met were having none of it, there were loads of Cardiff still trying to get in and only a few turnstiles were open. As things started to get a bit heavy outside, the police started directing City fans into the side stand. Now I know that Fulham usually have a few boys in that bit of the ground, so we made our way around and went in that section. When we got in, there were a fair few Cardiff lads there already. We didn't want to get noticed and taken out, so we kept apart. We'd been in this situation so many times, but had never had it handed to us on a plate by the police before!

The Cardiff end was packed solid and the police and stewards were coming in for a bit of verbal. We like to wait for an early goal before kicking things off – if not, it would be at half-time – but the Fulham lads were onto a few of our boys straightaway and that was that. I don't think the Fulham lads realised how many of us there were in there, but we all steamed in to help our lads out and they did the off. All the lads behind the goal saw this and were over the fences straightaway and onto the pitch, heading for the home end. That is a fantastic sight, seeing all your lads steaming across the pitch, taking a place over. The ref had to stop the game and he took the players off. The Fulham lot didn't want to know and the City fans just hung around on the pitch, having a laugh and enjoying the piss-take. Then the police came in, big style. They had the horses on the pitch and about 50 officers chasing everybody off. Once they got everyone off the pitch, and us in the corner and under control, they really started to give it some and hit out at anyone they could. That's fucking stupid, that is, because the fighting was over by then and they were just kicking it all off again and winding people up. It was them that put us in there in the first place anyway. The police never seem to understand that once it's done, it's done. We'd taken Fulham, we'd finished as far as the match and the ground were concerned.

Once again, Cardiff and Wales had come to town and kicked the arse of the mouthy, English, Cockney prats.

All we can say after that is that one good turn deserves another. What is amazing is just how much bottle some people have in returning the favour.

SLAYING THE DRAGON . . . WELL, SORT OF

Leyton Orient seem to be every Londoner's favourite other team. We get back-up from Yids, Irons and Gooners whenever a reputation is due to visit Brisbane Road. All very handy, but we also have a few regulars of our own that turn out home and away. There are a few little mobs, the Silly Donuts, West Side Alcoholics, the Shoe Crew and the Frog Squad, but we haven't got the numbers to go looking for it. Mind you, if anyone thinks they can come down and just take liberties then they will get an unwelcome surprise.

Cardiff always come down in numbers looking to kick it off. Last time was a riot with two Taffies getting stabbed at Leyton station, but on the day they did the business. A couple of our lads got well turned-over, one having a brick whacked on his head as he lay on the deck. Out of order, but it happens if you play the game. He was off work for a week and it nearly cost him his job. After something like that you look for a bit of payback, so next time they were down we were looking to even the score. It's not only the top firms that organise their hits.

One of our lads was born in Merthyr Tydfil and hated Cardiff with a passion, so armed with some local know-ledge, a Merthyr shirt (!) and two mates, he went to Paddington to hook up with the Soul Crew as they arrived in town. He told the Taffies that he was an exiled Bluebird and that the two lads were along for the piss-up, didn't like football and probably wouldn't go to the game.

Most fans coming to London like to hit the West End and make a day of it. We were waiting in the Hope pub in Tottenham Street for the call from our lads, to let us know the score with this lot and if it was possible to hit. We got the call, saying that their mob had split up to do the shopping bit and that our lads were sitting in the Dog and Trumpet in Carnaby Street with about 20 Cardiff, having a beer. To get away and make the call, one of our lads told them that he was going to become an adopted Bluebird for the day and was going into the football shop opposite to get a Cardiff scarf – clever.

The twelve of us were all carrying bottles and glasses tucked in our jackets. When we got close, we sent one of the lads around to scout the place, go inside to check the numbers, pretend to make a call and get the nod from our boys. He came back pretty sharpish: the Taffies were all drinking outside, our lads knew the score and the time to hit was now. We went around in twos and threes, mixing in with the shoppers but keeping close to the pub.

Our lad in the Merthyr top kicked it off. He walked to the front of the Taffies and shouted 'Orient' at the top of his voice. He cracked his bottle right on the nose of this guy, who went down like a log. They hadn't a fucking clue what was about to happen. We let them have the bottles and that, then steamed in. The shoppers ran like fuck and most of the Taffies ran back in the pub. Then there was the old stand-off before a few of their lads started to have a go back. They didn't do bad at standing their ground and it was some show for the tourists. Then the blades started to come out and that forced the stand-off. Some of their lads were more than ready to pay back the stabbings at Leyton station if we steamed in again. We fucked off pretty quick as the police around there are well sharp, but this had been a lovely little hit and we had taken them well by surprise.

Ten minutes later we were all back in the Hope, full of it and lining up the drinks for the three lads that set the Taffies up. At the match, the police were out in force. I think word had got around about the hit and it was obvious the Cardiff lads were giving it the large one to pay this back there and then. Didn't happen, though.

Brentford have always found it hard to shake off the tag of having Chelsea fans do their fighting for them. From personal experience we know that while on occasions this has certainly been the case, on others they have undertaken their own dirty work. As we have

always said, it only takes a few blokes to make a firm. These lads
from Exeter found themselves stung by a particularly nasty group
of Bees.

NASTY LITTLE Bs

We don't get that much trouble with the London firms, but
if it is going to happen then it's most likely to come down
with Brentford.

The first time they came looking for it was a couple of
years back. A couple of our lads were out having a look
around when they came across a few Brentford lads sitting
outside a pub. They walked past a couple of times, to see if
there were more inside, when the Brentford boys clocked
what was going on and started taking the piss, saying that
we would need a lot more than a few little boys to scare
them off. Our lads stopped to have a go back and then one
of the Brentford lads got up, walked over and asked if they
were serious. When our lad told him we had a few lads
and where they could find us, the Brentford lad punched
him straight in the mouth and told him to fuck off, saying it
was our patch and it was down to us to go looking for them.
Our lads ran straight down to our pub to give us the news
and so off we went, about fifteen of us.

As we marched up to the pub, we could see the same
five lads sitting outside and they soon see us coming. They
sat and watched us get closer and there was no fucking
about, we crossed the road and ran straight at them. These
lads got straight up, lobbed their glasses at us and steamed
in as well. Fair play to them, they went for it. Then from
out of the pub came another ten or twelve of them, only
this lot were well tooled-up. Two of the lads had what
looked like bike-chains and were swinging them around
their heads; another one had a claw-hammer. They were
going mental and were totally up for it, real nutters. They
chased us off down the road, then went back to the pub – I
think they must have thought we were leading them into

something. We mobbed-up again and were slowly starting to get tooled-up with what we could find when the Old Bill promptly arrived, went straight for us and nicked two of our lads for carrying offensive weapons.

We only get small gates at Exeter but we have a decent little firm of 50 or so lads, more than ready to have a go if some team comes looking for it in our town. We could see these lads in their end during the game, but they didn't look to have much else in the way of lads. As the match went on, word soon spread: we would go off in small groups to avoid the police, get tooled up, meet in one of the sidestreets then head straight back to the pub where they had been.

They had already turned up and were just getting into their minibuses when we steamed in and let them have it. They had no weapons this time and we had a top row with them. They gave a good account of themselves considering the numbers, but their buses were well fucked. It was going to be a long, cold journey home without any window screens. The police turned up and got them back into the car park. We were waiting on the other side of the road. There was loads of verbal going on, and a few of them were still trying to get out and have a go at us. We just stood taking the piss, telling the police to let them go. Once more police arrived, they moved us off back down to the city centre.

The next year we were expecting more of the same. Before the game, we checked out the same pub and a few others but didn't find anyone, just a few scarfers. It looked like they had bottled out after what happened before.

After the game, we made our way around to their end and again there was nothing happening, just knobs getting onto coaches and mums and dads, that's all; so it was back up to the centre for a few beers. We were walking up the main drag when from out of a side-road came these ten blokes going ape-shit. It was some of the same lads from the year before and they were out to prove a point. They had obviously been waiting for us and they wanted it, big time.

This time they didn't seem to have any tools but took us completely by surprise. They were well outnumbered but they didn't give a toss as they went for it, chasing our lads all over the place. They were clever though, because they kept close to each other so that none of them got cornered off. After sussing things out, we steamed back and had a massive ruck. It was going off in the middle of the road and in people's gardens, face-to-face knocking the shit out of each other, a good honest ruck. They were mad for it though, and to be honest they were well on top. Then one of our lads got tripped up and fell under a car that was trying to get away. It drove right over his leg. It looked horrible and he was screaming like I've never heard before. The Brentford lads backed off so we could get him out of the road, and the whole thing just stopped. As we tried to get our mate sorted out, they did the off up towards the centre, leaving us to it. Our mate's leg was broken in two places, so fair play to them for stopping. I've always been a bit iffy about going to Brentford since then, but on the couple of times I have been there I haven't seen any of these lads – and I don't really want to.

Wimbledon Football Club have hit the headlines for many reasons over the years, but unlike the rest of the London teams those reasons have never included crowd violence, so hats off to their supporters for that achievement. We would imagine that most of you expected this club to draw a blank within the pages of this book and yes, so did we. It was hard, admittedly, but nonetheless two stories did come to light. The first came from Jay in the Midlands.

BAGGING A WOMBLE

When I was fourteen, I travelled to Plough Lane with my Dad on the West Brom supporters' coach for an FA Cup match. Wimbledon was supposed to be the safest place to visit in the country but when we arrived, everyone was talking about a massive fight that had gone on before the game in the town centre, as the rival fans clashed. The team were well beaten on the day and as we made our way back to the coaches, we could see loads of our fans getting together before they moved off towards the town.

My Dad wanted me on the coach and out of the way as soon as possible. As the coaches moved off, we could see all these people come running back around the corner and there was loads of shouting. One of the coaches in front had been hit by some bricks and the windows had gone through. I could see all these lads getting off the coach and steaming up the road. As we pulled across the junction, the coach stopped and this lad got on, shouting that the Wimbledon lads had got mobbed-up and were throwing bricks at Albion fans. All these blokes on our coach got off as well, and the last we saw of them was as they ran up the road to join the mob. There were loads of things flying through the air and a couple of police on horses in the middle of the road, charging about.

The coach moved off and stopped a few miles up the road along with all the others. That was my first experience of football violence; I didn't expect it to happen at Wimbledon.

Dave from Richmond told us the following story. Although not a particularly violent incident, it shows just how pathetic the hooligans can get.

NONE TOO SAINTLY

We were playing down at Southampton in a league match and, as usual, I travelled down by train with another four regulars. We set off from Waterloo and there were about 50 other faces we knew on the train as well. One group of six lads were obviously on for a big day out, and even though it was only about ten in the morning they already seemed pretty drunk.

We were all having a laugh and these lads were singing away when the train stopped at Basingstoke. Into the carriage came these four lads, all about 20 and wearing Saints shirts. We gave them a jeer but they took it as it was meant and started laughing. After about ten minutes, one of the loud Wimbledon lads got up to go to the toilet. I can honestly say I've never seen him before or since and he was massive. As he walked past the Southampton lads, he called them all wankers and the whole carriage went quiet. When he came back all eyes were on him and again he called the Southampton lads wankers, but this time he stopped by them. They all laughed, then he told them to tell him what they were.

One of their lads, who must have seen this sort of thing happen over and over again, tried to humour the moron: 'We're wankers, mate, top-drawer wankers.' The moron was swaying, hardly able to stand thanks to the train moving about, and couldn't make out what to do next when two of his mates joined him and asked what was going on. He told his mate that the Saints fans were 'wankers', to which his mate said, 'Oh, is that right?' and started hitting one of these lads in the head. The other three morons came over and joined in as well, then some other Dons fans moved in to help these Southampton lads out and break it up. One of them had his lip split, just for following another team, it's pathetic. The whole mood for the day was changed and as they were led to the safety of another coach by this woman and her son, the moron shouted out after them one last time, 'Don't forget, you're fucking wankers, right?' It was almost laughable.

As each club continues the battle to rid themselves of the hooligan problem, they must ask themselves if they are just shifting the violence to another arena. If it is simply a case of 'Not at our club' being good enough, then football as a whole will never rid itself of the hooligans.

CAPITAL PUNISHMENT

BARNET

Well done lads, a clean sheet.

Chapter 16
Amateur Dramatics

For any football fan, the ultimate sin is to give up on your team and start supporting another club. No matter how bad it gets – and let's face it, for most of us it's bad because there can only be so many winners – you can't just turn to a more successful side and hope to be accepted. We all have our cross to bear, and for most of us that cross is the football club we support.

However, there is one option open that is in a way acceptable: the local non-league side. I really enjoy going to non-league games. I like the people, the grounds, the football's good and the food's always better. It never makes me feel like I am being unfaithful, although after following the rise of both Barnet and Wycombe at home and away games, I was forced to stop the moment each club gained league status. Overnight they became rivals, and local rivals at that. Of course, football at non-league level is not without its problems, and although I would never have got involved in another mob's argument, I did witness disturbances at both these clubs.

As the supporters of the London league clubs cover such a vast catchment area, the hooligan firms find themselves dotted around the suburbs and New Towns. When their local side has a big game, the violent element will often latch on to the big day and bring problems to a usually friendly club.

Hayes in Middlesex were once drawn to play away at

Stevenage Borough in the FA Cup. The Hertfordshire club do have a reputation for being a bit mouthy and during the game at Borough's Broadhall Way stadium the Hayes fans had to put up with a fair bit of verbal, as well as threats outside afterwards when a few punches were thrown. In the return game, the story was quite different. Word had got around that Stevenage had a fair little mob and fancied themselves a bit, and this brought the local Hayes lads out in force.

The atmosphere had been boiling up all night as the local lads massed as close to the Stevenage supporters as they could, intimidating and abusing them throughout the game. Following the second Stevenage goal, the local lads charged across the terrace into the Borough fans, forcing them to do a runner as the police lost control. This was like watching old footage from the seventies as fans scattered across the terraces and panic set in. There were lads and police on the pitch, and the image of a police officer and a shocked steward holding on to a handcuffed fan by the halfway line was something that appeared in many newspapers the next day.

Hayes Football Club stated that those involved were not regular Hayes supporters, just local lads out to spoil the night and gain revenge for an incident that had occurred after the first match, but unfortunately this wasn't the first time that such an incident had taken place at their ground. When Swansea City came to play in the same competition a few seasons earlier, seventeen fans were arrested and many others ejected as fighting broke out during the match. It was believed that supporters from Chelsea, Millwall, West Ham and QPR were all involved.

FA Cup fixtures always have the effect of tempting the local lads out under the banner of putting their town on the map. For many experienced hooligans, the opportunity to play up at a ground where the stewards and the police have no idea what to expect is something that is too good to miss. The fact that there will almost certainly be no CCTV in place to film them is an added bonus. It must be said that these people are highly unlikely to be regular supporters at the club, but unfortunately for the team concerned, this image is likely to stick and when the next big game comes along, the opposition will have their violent following turn out and the whole thing starts to snowball.

When Woking were drawn to play Millwall at home in the FA Cup, most of those involved in the running of the club must have taken a sharp intake of breath, but for the local head-cases this was the best possible result. Woking are one of the best-supported non-league sides in the country. Their home fixtures enjoy bigger crowds than some of those in the Second Division and their away following would be the envy of many league sides. The club is extremely well run and their supporters, although very vocal, are not known to play up.

The match ended in a draw, but during the game it became clear that the home support had been bolstered by a large number of fans that were ready to give the Millwall followers a run for their money. At the final whistle, the Millwall fans were kept behind for a short time which enabled the locals to firm up and get around to the Millwall end of the ground. As the visiting fans were let out into the car park, they were met by a large mob baiting them forward.

WOKING

I mean, fucking Woking for Christ's sake. They were mostly young lads that had probably never seen anything like this before in their lives. They would have run a mile if things had gone off. There were a few lads I recognised from one of the top London firms and they seemed to be at the centre of it all. We knew they lived in this area and had expected a few to turn out, but they had pulled a few of their mates in as well. Everyone wants a pop at Millwall these days, but let's get real: they threw a few things, then fucked off as soon as the coppers started to get a bit heavy. That will be enough for them – 'We had a go at Millwall' and all that – but I tell you what, if we have to come down here again, we'll fucking wreck the place. They won't get away with that again.

During the Surrey Senior Cup final, the Woking fans found

themselves on the receiving end when supporters from Tooting and Mitcham held up the kick-off for ten minutes following a pitch invasion. Police reinforcements were called in and the Woking manager had to restrain one supporter about to use the corner flag as a javelin. That season, the Tooting fans' reputation went before them and following an attempt to 'take' the Aldershot end, their little mob were attacked at the train station.

When Basildon United lost at home to Raunds in the FA Vase in 1995, some home fans attacked their visitors. As they tried to escape, some were chased down the players' tunnel. The total crowd was 699, away fans numbered 300 and the police presence was one. Most of those involved were reported to be wearing West Ham shirts and they had attacked the visitors from both sides, suggesting that the incident had been planned in advance.

When incidents like this happen, the non-league clubs go on the defensive by offering up the usual 'We have never seen these people here before, they are not supporters of this football club' excuses. We would not argue with that, because for the majority it is almost certainly true. The problem is that as the word spreads, those involved may just take a liking to the reputation they have brought upon their little club, and as the big boys continue to price people away from *their* game, the hooligans will start to look for an alternative place in which to indulge their craving for violence. That is why the attitude of 'Not on my doorstep' simply places the problem somewhere else. It won't make it go away.

These incidents are only the tip of the iceberg as Romford, Tilbury, Canvey Island and Borehamwood have all had their problems in recent years, some of which continue to this day. Those in charge of football at all levels must heed the warning: the local non-league side offers an acceptable alternative for the hooligan. If they don't take notice, then sooner or later these clubs will find themselves in serious trouble.

As the top clubs, not content with bleeding their own domestic market dry, try to seek out a new worldwide clientele, Craig D. has spotted an opening that just might see an unlikely candidate for England's 'World League' representatives.

LONDON 1, NEW YORK CITY 0

The Pepsi Max World League of Football is on its way, folks, and why not? Don't fight it, think about it: London v Glasgow, Amsterdam v London, Munich, Rome, Rio – that is some impressive fixture list and the crowd-pulling potential is massive. You can't deny it, football in the lower leagues is finished. It's bollocks to think it, I know, but it's true. If you had a choice of Palace v Reading in the Frank's Café Second Division South Group C or London v Madrid at a new super-stadium, what would it be? Well, ask yourself. Believe me, it's going to happen, you can see it every season as UEFA restructure the European competitions. It's what the big clubs want, where the money is – but do they realise they can't *all* have it? What about the Arsenal, Spurs, Chelsea, etc? Just big fish in a small pond, I'm afraid. Think of the money to be made, and money talks. Football is now the global game and the top players will go after that top money. As for the likes of Orient and Fulham . . . well, I'm sorry but it's over, and I really am sorry because my club may just go the same way. People have short memories, remember Maidstone United? Exactly. Don't think that they weren't just as important to a small group of people in Kent, and what did you do for them? Fuck all, matey.

You see, unless you actually support West Ham, Charlton or Brentford, no one else actually gives a fuck. Those that do follow them would never give up the name, the history or their loyalty to that club, or be able to stand shoulder-to-shoulder with the supporters of their darkest rivals, but for me there may be an answer, a way out. I am lucky because I follow the one London club that could possibly pull this off. You see, Wimbledon are harmless. Apparently we have no fans (?), no home, and play crap football that no one wants to watch (?). We have no real fan-hatred with another club and are always seen as the underdogs, and that has people on your side.

Sod moving to Dublin, Milton Keynes or Outer Mongolia.

Bollocks to the local council, this is the biggest opportunity any club could ever have and it's right here in front of our noses. You may think it ridiculous, Wimbledon representing what in effect would be England, but by the time it was up and running most of you wouldn't recognise it as Wimbledon. A different name, possibly our own new stadium, a new team, *survival*. Yes, Sammy would be our leader, Vinny could be our public relations officer and we would of course still be known as the Dons, and that should be more than enough to satisfy our existing fans. To us it would always be Wimbledon FC.

The possibilities of this are endless and the more you think about it, the more the reality sinks in. Remember American football and their World League? Yeah, bollocks I know, but they had the vision and it nearly worked. Wembley was full, you can't tell me it wasn't because I was there. I actually liked the game until I saw it live, then I realised it was shit, along with 79,999 others. Just like Teenage Mutant Ninja Turtles it was an all-American fad, here today, gone tomorrow. Football isn't like that. Even the Americans have got it now, they know that football equals big bucks and America could become true world champions in a sport that is recognised outside the good old US of A. Ego-tastic, kids.

Imagine the top boys at FIFA headquarters rubbing their hands. A worldwide league consisting of just 16 teams, 30 games a season. The best talent in the world being beamed (pay-per-view, mind) direct into every bar, front-room and mud-hut in the world. Big, big money. World merchandising rights, multi-national sponsorship deals. It's frightening, all that money going to so few sides. Wouldn't that be divine justice to see Wimbledon, once selling the family silver just to survive, then creaming Liverpool and Newcastle of their greatest talent? Watching the Dons wave the chequebook. You know the saying, 'What goes around comes around.' Yeah: Merton, London, England, the World. I can see it now, happening before my eyes.

But hang on a minute, it won't work. Where are all the new fans going to come from? You don't just stop following your club side and go somewhere else, it's true. Well, that's OK, you can continue to watch Chelsea in the feeder leagues if you like, I couldn't give a fuck, enjoy. I'll watch my football live every Sunday, 7 p.m. (European time) at the Dickie Guy Stadium or via the TV. I may even take in the odd Saturday game just to remind myself what I'm missing, but if you think that there aren't another 40,000 like me then wake up, sleepy head, this is London: population 8,500,000 and growing.

Ten years ago you would never have seen a kid wearing a Man United strip in the East End, but live football has changed all that. Families that would once have been Arsenal through and through, generation after generation, now find there are Newcastle, Liverpool, even Everton fans living under the same roof. You can't take your kid down to Stamford Bridge if he or she insists on wearing their favourite Aston Villa shirt, can you? So the kids stay at home and wait to watch *Match of the Day* or Sky.

Remember dreaming about taking your son down Loftus Road? Now he taunts you about following a bag of shite, then asks you to tape Southampton v Coventry. Aahhhh! Wouldn't it be lovely to go together as a family? Well, roll up, roll up, here's your chance; grab it by the bollocks and go for it. This could save your marriage, mend the relation-ship with your children, make you a 'new man'. There are loads of football fans in London that don't find themselves attached to any club, and there will be loads more when the smaller ones start to go under. All those trendy fans that followed England during Euro 96, the boyfriend–girlfriend terrace lovers, will suddenly have a team playing league football, football with meaning and passion, week after week and not every two years (if we're lucky). Unlike following the England side, this could become a habit if it's always on offer.

Let's face it, your club has treated you like dirt over the

last five or six years. Ticket prices, travel to away games, merchandise, food – the list is endless, but at least you would know where you stood from the start. Take a look at your club; admit it, it's not like the good old days. You don't stand in the wind and rain, you don't worry quite so much about the walk back to the train station or having your coach bricked. Cold pies, funny-tasting tea, not being able to see the corner flag and having fences blocking out half of the pitch. For the new breed of fan all those things are impossible to understand, but for many that *was* football, and at the risk of sounding like some old git, it's the way many want to remember it. That is why so many people have stayed away, as if not wanting to go to a funeral wake: for them, football died a long time ago. An awful lot of people would rather remember it the way it was, and I totally understand that.

I would imagine there'd be a few divisions, with the likes of Manchester and Hamburg in the lower reaches, but FIFA would insist on London having the initial starting opportunity and why not, I say. The financial backers, coaches and players would be climbing over themselves to be part of it. Money, money, money. In the end it rules, OK.

It's amazing that FIFA haven't done something similar with the national sides. They could scrap the World Cup and turn it into a league, played over four seasons with relegation and promotion. Surely the greedy bastards at every governing body throughout the planet have thought of the freebies to be had? Maybe it's the thought of Italy, Germany and England not quite having enough quality for the likes of Brazil, Croatia or Nigeria, and we couldn't have that. So three cheers for FIFA, Nigeria and London FC. Hip, hip, hooray for Sky and global TV. That reminds me, I must remember to set the video for 'The English League Goal Fest' programme on Tuesday mornings at 1.45 a.m. I must check who's playing for Palace these days and have a little laugh to myself. Me, I'll be safely tucked up dreaming about Lisbon at home this coming Sunday.

CONCLUSION

_____

**Stockport
When Jimmy Hill Was Right**

Conclusion

Throughout this book, as with our other books, we have included a number of accounts of violence involving football fans from all over the country. These were obtained through interviews, or sent to us by genuine football fans, and have, as always, been recounted verbatim. Because they are so graphic, we hope that they will shock people into taking a step back themselves and realising just what could happen if they were to turn up at the wrong street at the wrong time. But the sad truth is that what we have included is just a sample of what is sent to us, and many of the more violent incidents are excluded because, frankly, they defy belief. Despite this, we still meet numerous people who insist on telling us that football violence is a thing of the past, hopefully, and thankfully, never to be seen again. These people accuse us of glorifying violence, of offering no solutions to the problem (which they insist does not exist) and of raking up the past in order to sell a few books to the brain-dead people that were once killing the game – the very same hooligans that kept decent, innocent people away from the stadiums. While we would agree with the last part of that statement, the rest is total bollocks.

We believe we do not glorify violence, merely tell it like it is in order to make people understand what drives football hooligans into fighting at football. It is violent, it is ugly and it does scare the shit out of you when someone pulls a knife out and waves it around in front of your face. Indeed, it was such an incident that made us stand back, take a good look at ourselves, and ultimately stop fighting at games ourselves. Yes, it is true that we live in a violent society, but the difference between football-related violence and the threat of someone smashing a glass in your face down the local pub is that the football club, for the hooligan, provides a focal point and, ultimately, something to defend. The sad truth is that many people will set out to a match with just that in mind, while others will be planning to attack that club through its supporters. They will have thought things through, been in contact with the opposition, planned a meeting with another firm in order to fight. It is those aspects that make football violence different from any everyday violence that most of us come across at some time in our lives. It is also the very reason why it remains a football problem, rather than society's and, until those in charge take note of that and get their house in order, we will continue to do all we can to expose the background and continuing existence of this problem. The argument that football is not responsible for its fans fighting outside stadia is ridiculous. If fans from Chelsea travel to Leicester and fight in the city centre on the day that Chelsea play Leicester, then that has to be a football problem. Not only are they fighting under the name of football, but they are hopefully prevented from doing so by police paid for by football, and their actions drag the name of football down into the gutter. Such violence affects football, so it must be a football problem and no one will ever convince us otherwise.

Those who say that football violence has long since disappeared should take a quick reality check. In January 1997, Millwall travelled to play Stockport County at Edgeley Park. Stockport's hooligan following have earned themselves a growing reputation over the last few seasons – something that hadn't gone unnoticed in South-East London. A. H. from Preston attended the match at the request of some of the Stockport faithful.

* * *

Conclusion

STOCKPORT

It is true that I went to the match in the hope of seeing, and possibly getting involved in, some trouble. I don't follow County but I know a few of their lads and they had invited me down as they were ready to have a go at the Millwall. They had been waiting all season for this one. I've come across Millwall a few times up at Preston, but I couldn't believe what went on here.

The police and the Stockport lads weren't ready for this and it really makes you wonder what it's like when Millwall go for it with the numbers. County had a good firm out and they were ready to give it a go, but I came across the Millwall lads early on and once I'd seen what they had out, I decided to take the option of being a keen observer. After all, it wasn't my team involved.

The London firms always seem to be made up of blokes rather than lads, and this lot looked well nasty. The place had a really hostile atmosphere before the match, but I didn't hear of anything happening. It seemed that the locals were just mobbing-up and sussing things out and the Millwall lads were letting them know they were there and giving the County firm the chance to prove themselves. As usual, it was up to the home lads to kick things off but nothing happened outside, although once we got into the ground, things started to turn.

At County the away fans still share the toilets with the home fans and stories were coming back that the Millwall lads, after seeing their team play shit, were ready to get things on with the locals. Rumours were coming back that there were knives being flashed around and the police were still trying to suss things out but didn't know what to do. They certainly didn't seem to have the numbers to do much in any case. In fact, the Millwall lads could really have done some damage and kicked it off big time if they had wanted to.

After the match, we made our way onto the main road

237

and waited to see what was happening. The Millwall lads had made their way back towards the pub they had used earlier and the County fans were mobbing-up at their local. One of the County lads came up to us on a scouting mission and, as we stood talking, some of the Millwall blokes came around the corner and walked towards us. One of them was saying that he was QPR's main man, he was really buzzing and it was obvious that he was mad for it, wanting to know where the County lads were and all that stuff. I told him I was just down watching and the County fan told him what pub they were in, and off he went. If he was shitting himself, he certainly covered it well. It never fails to amaze me how lads will talk to each other and line things up nowadays.

The Millwall mob were starting to get really edgy and were obviously telling this lad to go and tell the County firm that it was their move, as they were at home, when suddenly out came a knife from one of the Londoners and he was shouting that they should just slice us up there and then because County had shit out and they hadn't come all this way for nothing. Out came another couple of blades as we jumped back over the wall and the police, who had been watching what was going on, came flying down the road as they thought things were kicking off. The blades were put away before they got there and, as ever, nobody grassed anyone up. There you are with someone seriously about to scar you for life and you don't grass him, mad really. That was it; I was off. I heard later that the police caught up with the Millwall lads, brought more people in and got them out of town as soon as possible but they scared the shit out of me. They were mental.

While it is clear that the police, and to a certain extent the local mob, were not expecting Millwall to turn up with such a hardcore firm, of greater interest is the fact that lads from other London firms were present within the Millwall ranks. This seems to be on the increase of late, possibly due to the fact that the flexible fixture lists demanded by television leave a lot of football fans without a live game to watch. As members of various organised firms make more frequent contact with each other it is inevitable that friendships will form and invitations to travel will be extended. To the outsider it may seem odd (to say the least) that people who sometimes indulge in violence with each other can get along at all, but this merely reinforces the fact that football violence is a very strange phenomenon.

The weekend after the Millwall–Stockport incident was FA Cup fourth round day and on the Saturday Barnsley were playing at QPR. The Yorkshire side have another firm with a growing reputation and, as we have heard throughout this book, a visit to London provides a big day out for many supporters. As a small group of 15 of their main lads drank in Covent Garden they found themselves the victims of a vicious attack from a mob of around 30 West Ham fans. At first the Yorkshiremen fancied their chances with this mob, and thus building their own reputation even higher, but they waited too long. Once the West Ham lads had mobbed-up it became clear that they were getting too out-numbered to handle it. The landlord of the pub, apparently worried about damage to his bar, offered them what they thought was an escape route through the back door but unfortunately for them, the escape route offered led directly into a dead end where they were ambushed and given a serious hiding. It would seem that West Ham are back on the case.

The following day Chelsea played Liverpool at Stamford Bridge in what was an epic game. As the nation watched the game live on TV and enjoyed the atmosphere generated, they remained blissfully unaware that the firms attached to both clubs had arranged a meeting at Victoria station prior to kick-off, a rerun of a clash between the two sets of fans earlier in the season.

In February, Millwall played host to their old rivals Bristol City. In the days leading up to this fixture it was announced that the London club were in serious financial trouble and this only added to the tension surrounding the match. The City firm came out in full force and before the match were involved in various incidents giving fair warning that they were more than willing to take Millwall on. Throughout the match small skirmishes broke out, but on the final whistle the Millwall fans invaded the pitch. The two firms, intent on trouble, were desperate to get at each other and seats were ripped out and used as weapons by both sets of hooligans. The Millwall chairman suggested on BBC Radio 5 that the violence between the two sets of fans had actually been a pitch invasion to demonstrate against the board and the financial situation the club had suddenly found itself in. Fans from both clubs rang in to give their accounts of what had happened and eventually he accused the Bristol fans of ripping out the seats and throwing them at the Millwall fans.

Following on from their victory over Liverpool in the FA Cup Chelsea were drawn to play away at Leicester City. Once again the BBC elected to televise the game live, so the violence that took place was brought into the living-rooms all over the country. As the half-time whistle went the BBC panel of experts, before discussing the actual match, highlighted the crowd problems that were occurring right beneath their gantry. Jimmy Hill said that the problem had clearly never gone away and that football was fooling itself and the supporters if it continued to ignore the fact. S. H. explains how he saw the incident.

WHEN JIMMY HILL WAS RIGHT

Just after Chelsea scored their first goal, a group of Chelsea lads jumped up cheering in the main stand, which was full of City fans. In all there must have been about 50 Chelsea in there, but this group of about 16 were up for standing their corner if trouble started. God only knows how they got their tickets as this is a home-fans-only stand. They were being a bit mouthy from the start, but once they scored that wound up the City lads no end. We don't get on with Chelsea at the best of times, but with this being such a big game it made it worse and a lot of the City lads made their way over to the corner to join in. I've never been a fan of seats and this is where they can be really dangerous, for if trouble starts it's very hard to move away and if you were to fall down you would be in real danger of getting crushed. It started to get really heated, then Chelsea scored again. These lads were really taking the piss, so a few punches got thrown and all hell breaks out as seats are ripped out and thrown by both sets of fans. I remember thinking that the whole country would be seeing this and that Leicester would be banned just because of a few idiots.

I watched the game on video when I got home and, thankfully, they didn't show it at all, but to say there were only a handful of seats thrown was wrong, there must've been at least 100 seats on the pitch. Those that threw them should be banned by the clubs for life. If just one of those seats had hit someone it could have scarred them for life and these idiots don't care who gets hurt as there were plenty of kids in that area.

Trouble continued after the match, with one group of Chelsea fans locked in a pub as the local lads looked to gain revenge for what was an incident started by just a handful of people. However, it is clear to us that this incident could have been avoided if segregation had been fully achieved and if the stewards on the ground had acted quickly to remove the Chelsea fans from that area. Something obviously went wrong at this volatile fixture and in the long term it could have cost Leicester a lot more than an FA inquiry. However, it was no isolated incident. Trouble broke out at most of the Cup ties that day, with 60 arrests at the Sheffield Wednesday–Bradford game, 34 at the Chesterfield–Forest game and two massive offs in Leeds city centre involving Portsmouth supporters.

The replay of the Chelsea–Leicester game at Stamford Bridge was also marred by disturbances outside the stadium before and after the match while Chelsea's next tie, at Portsmouth, saw over 300 supporters from both clubs fighting in the morning of the match at Southsea, a meeting arranged days in advance of the actual game.

On Saturday 22 March 1997 Portsmouth came to London to play QPR at Loftus Road. The Pompey firm, the 657, were originally in town for another pre-arranged meeting with Chelsea lads but the police were on top of the situation and thankfully kept the two groups apart. Unfortunately, the police escorted the Pompey lads to Loftus Road and allowed them to enter the ground in an area away from the main Portsmouth end, including a number in the family enclosure. The fighting started first in the Ellerslie Road stand and then in the South Africa Road stand causing other supporters to leave the stands and move onto the pitch, forcing the players off the field for almost twenty minutes. This incident should have sent shivers down the spine of those at Lancaster Gate because it was clear that the Pompey firm tried to 'take' the QPR home end. Something that many, including us, believed was a thing of the past. It was also clear that the resulting trouble not only demonstrated that the threat of CCTV was being totally ignored, but that the Pompey hooligans were prepared to start their attack from a family enclosure full of women and children. Once again questions must also be asked as to how 30 lads can purchase tickets for such an area of the stadium in the first place.

All the incidents listed above happened in the ten-week period at the beginning of 1997 and, as you may have noticed, all include London clubs. Sadly, the few incidents mentioned here merely scratch the surface of what actually happened during that period. Yet while incidents involving supporters continue to happen both outside, and increasingly inside, grounds every week, things have taken a more sinister turn as an added ingredient has entered the fray: attacks on players and referees.

Recent examples of this have taken place at Wolves, Millwall, Barnsley, Leeds and Sheffield United, but the worst took place at Brighton during the Leyton Orient fixture. Following a late Orient goal, a small number of Brighton fans got onto the pitch and actually attacked the Orient players after the goalscorer allegedly made gestures at the Brighton fans. While there is no doubt that those involved should have been banned from all football for life, as well as being dealt with by the courts, it is clear that the club should also have been held to account over this incident, which should, ultimately, have cost them everything. While the FA failed to come down heavily on Brighton, and the fans will be at the mercy of the courts, the FA must be seen to take action against players whose behaviour can provoke the fans. Too often players act in such a manner towards the fans, yet they rarely find themselves punished.

This problem was never more clearly demonstrated than in the aftermath of a flare-up between Chesterfield and Plymouth players towards the end of their league fixture. This incident undoubtedly helped spark violence between the two sets of fans. Yet the police, despite video evidence, have announced that no action shall be taken against those players involved. In contrast, those supporters arrested that day will (quite rightly) find no such leniency when they appear before the local magistrates. What kind of message does this send out to the players and the spectators? What will it take to make the police and FA act? If there is a brawl on the pitch surely criminal action should be taken against the individuals involved. Similarly, if there is evidence of racial abuse against fellow professionals it should be punished. How else can the FA claim to be putting its weight behind the campaign to get rid of racists in the stands? Double standards, suggesting that players are somehow above the law, make the game a laughing stock and smacks of weak leadership.

We have admitted that we were once involved in football violence, but thankfully our participation ended back in 1988. However, as people who know what it is like to be involved in hooliganism, we feel that we can bring an insight to this issue that no one else seems willing to do. We haven't studied it from a distance, or carried out exhaustive social studies, or used participant observations; we were actually a part of it. We are not proud of that, but it enables us to understand what drives these people and gives us the ability to see the all-too-clear danger signs. Similarly, we believe that our background gives us a greater authority on the subject than those who have no experience of hooliganism at first hand. When we wrote *Everywhere We Go*, we naively hoped that by exposing the fact that the problem had never been away and was once again on the increase, the authorities would act. After all, forewarned is forearmed. Yet, even after we wrote *England, My England* to highlight the problems caused by English fans in the past and faced by them in recent years (as Manchester United fans who travelled to FC Porto will willingly testify), nothing appears to have been done and no one within the game appears to be taking this issue seriously. For those people who say that we have brought nothing to the debate we simply say read carefully the accounts of those involved, because many of the answers to this problem are there if you open your eyes.

However, we believe our own suggestions may well work to help prevent hooliganism. As we have seen at recent games, the major deterrent offered by CCTV is no longer seen to be effective by the hooligans, as the threatened follow-up action rarely takes place. After spending so much money on the equipment, it seems ridiculous to us that the clubs and the police fail to use their greatest weapon to maximum effect. This seems doubly strange as most clubs know the names and faces involved at their ground and they have the power to ban them for life if caught. Believe us, once the word gets around that the clubs are banning people, and strictly enforcing those bans, things will improve.

The police, who cost the game so much money, must be seen to enforce the restriction orders placed upon convicted fans, just as they must enforce the rules ordering offenders to report to police stations on matchdays. When supporters point out potential troublemakers at games, the police must act to prevent any problems starting, rather than waiting for violence to break out before moving in. Groups of supporters who enter the wrong part of a stadium should be ejected and held until the match is finished, not taken around to their allocated end, where other like-minded fans will cheer them on as some kind of heroes. Furthermore, clubs should be held to account by the FA and the local licensing authorities when ticket arrangements have clearly been exploited and money in the bank becomes more important than crowd safety. If clubs cannot ensure the safety of their paying customers then they should not be given a safety certificate. Once one local authority enforces that particular rule, just watch how quickly every other club in the country sorts out that particular problem!

Conclusion

The worrying trend of fans running onto the pitch to celebrate goals is another issue that must be dealt with, primarily because the potential for an attack on a player or referee is so great. No one in their right mind would want to see the return of the fences but with so many new stadiums being built, surely other forms of deterrent, such as moats, should be considered or even made compulsory. It is much easier to control the visiting supporter, purely because of the lower numbers involved, but surely the loss of a few rows of seats at that part of the ground where they are to be housed is small price to pay to help that process. If visiting fans must be kept behind in a stadium after the match to enable the police to clear the area of the local head-cases, then keep them behind. There will always be supporters that moan about being locked in a ground after the final whistle but if it saves one fan getting attacked and makes the job of the police easier then it's worth it. In any case, those very same people will be the ones who shout the loudest when things go wrong and they personally feel intimidated.

There is nothing startlingly new here; all of these solutions sound simple and even obvious, but the best ideas always are. All the laws and equipment are already in place and yet the problem still exists, so maybe you should ask yourself where the reason for that lies. Of course, if people didn't want to fight at football there would be no problem; but the sad fact is that there is a small minority who do and that aspect has become so ingrained in football culture it will be difficult to remove. Yet the game has a duty to work towards changing those attitudes for the sake of the vast majority of decent fans who want to go to games in complete safety.

But the fact remains that the football hooligan still exists and the reason is that those who run our game still do not understand what makes him tick. The stereotypical unemployed racist skin-head thug from a broken home may well exist somewhere, but the vast majority of hooligans we talk to are reasonably intelligent blokes with decent jobs who see football as their thing. They are certainly not the complete idiots many people believe them to be, and for them the battle of wits with the police is just another part of the game. But because the game does not understand them, and therefore the problem, how can it hope to find a long-term cure?

It is easy to be reactive, but surely the time has come to be proactive and that can only be done by involving the average supporter in solving this matter. One of the main reasons that Charlton were so successful in combating violence associated with their club was down to the simple fact that the fans and the local community became actively involved in the relocation back to The Valley. If ever there was an example of what talking to the fans can achieve then this was it. It was the fans who got the club back at The Valley. The supporters were fed-up with how the club was handling the situation and with local government blocking every application, so they got together and forced people into action. Once the fans became involved, things started to happen and that gave the supporters of Charlton a sense of belonging. They had played their part in securing a return to their spiritual home and they wanted to look after what they had helped achieve – a safe place in which to enjoy their sport. If only more clubs would allow their fans to get involved, act on their opinions and then keep them involved.

There is, of course, another reason why the game should be working hard to deal with this problem. Not just for the safety of those who pay at the turnstiles, but for others who deal in a different kind of interest. With clubs seemingly rushing headlong into the stock exchange without a second thought, it seems doubtful if either the clubs or the FA have fully considered the consequences a major incident of hooliganism might have on a club's share price. The potential extends far beyond the loss of a few quid, because if things get really bad, a club could disappear overnight. Any club. Make no mistake, anything adverse that dragged a club from the back pages onto the front would have the City boys pulling out their money almost instantly, with the knock-on effect that a club's value would go through the floor overnight. Loyalty counts for nothing when money becomes involved. Yet it seems that the game is willing to gamble with this possibility and that is a very dangerous approach to take.

Conclusion

As long as the problem of hooliganism exists within the English game, we will continue to expose football's failure to deal with it. There is no doubt that the police and the FA are aware of what we have to say and they remain none too happy that we continue to say it, even seeing us as something of a thorn in their side. But this is something we find hard to understand – all we ever set out to do was make football wake up to the fact that it was in danger of shooting itself in the foot at a time when it appears to be riding the crest of a wave. We continue to get hassled whenever we attend matches away from our beloved Vicarage Road, despite the fact that we are not involved in football violence anymore.

We wrote these books for the simple reason that we were tired of watching people involved in football pretending to be putting the interests of the game before their own personal greed. There was no other motive, no great plan, it just happened. We are just two blokes who write about being football fans and we stand by every single word we write because we truly believe in what we say. The letters we receive every day from genuine supporters throughout Britain suggest that they agree with us. It is not that nice getting hassled by the police, or being continually branded an ex-hooligan on television or radio but if, through our writing, we finally force football into dealing with this problem then we feel we will have played our part and will have repaid a small piece of the debt we personally owe to the great game. We live in hope.

More Sport from Headline

everywhere we go

behind the matchday madness

dougie and eddy brimson

'Probably the best book ever written on football violence'
Daily Mail

'Offers a grim insight into the mind of the football thug'
Daily Mirror

'This honest, funny and refreshingly direct account achieves its aim of toppling a few careless stereotypes' *Independent on Sunday*

Written by two people who know the world of the hooligan from the inside, this bestselling book features many first-hand accounts of incidents, from both perpetrators and victims, that make chilling reading. It is the most comprehensive look at football violence and, among other subjects, explores:

* The changing face of hooliganism

* Who gets involved – and why

* How the 'firms' operate, both home and away

* The role of 'scouts' and 'spotters' in planning violence

* The football establishment – and how they can help solve the problem

NON-FICTION / SPORT 0 7472 5225 4

More Sport from Headline

england,
my england

the trouble with the national
football team

dougie and eddy brimson

'Quite simply brilliant' *Sky Sports Magazine*

'Fearlessly written . . . a thought-provoking read which
digs below the surface and explores the whole issue of
football violence' *Racing and Football Outlook*

Football violence, known everywhere as 'The English
Disease', is as widespread today as it has ever been.
England, My England is the book that finally exposes what
life is like among the most feared group of supporters in
the world – the England fans. Featuring first-hand
accounts of trips abroad, it explores many of the issues
and myths surrounding this subject, and explains why
some fans behave so differently when following their
country compared with their club.

NON-FICTION / SPORT 0 7472 5508 3

This book would not have been
possible without the help of football supporters
from all over the country.

If you have any views on the contents of this
book or would like to help us with our football-
related research please do not hesitate to
contact us at the address below.
We will add your name to our database
and send you regular questionnaires on
the issues that affect *you*, the
football supporter.

This is an opportunity to have your say.

All correspondence will be treated with the
utmost confidentiality.

Please write to:
Fandom
P.O. Box 766, Hemel Hempstead, Herts,
HP1 2TU